国防科技
保密机制比较研究

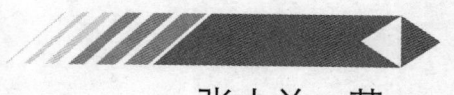

张小兰 著

中国财政经济出版社

图书在版编目（CIP）数据

国防科技保密机制比较研究/张小兰著.—北京：中国财政经济出版社，2008.5

ISBN 978 - 7 - 5095 - 0684 - 4

Ⅰ.国… Ⅱ.张… Ⅲ.国防科学技术 - 保密机制 - 比较研究 Ⅳ.E9

中国版本图书馆 CIP 数据核字（2008）第 063853 号

中国财政经济出版社出版

URL：http：//www.cfeph.cn

E - mail：cfeph @ cfeph.cn

（版权所有　翻印必究）

社址：北京市海淀区阜成路甲 28 号　邮政编码：100036
发行处电话：88190406　财经书店电话：64033436
北京牛山世兴印刷厂印刷　各地新华书店经销
880×1230 毫米　32 开　5.875 印张　140 000 字
2008 年 5 月第 1 版　2008 年 5 月北京第 1 次印刷
印数：1—2 000　定价：15.00 元
ISBN 978 - 7 - 5095 - 0684 - 4/F·0554
（图书出现印装问题，本社负责调换）

内 容 简 介

综合国力的竞争，归根到底是科技实力的竞争。在残酷的科技竞争中，科技窃密活动作为竞争对手取得竞争优势的重要手段，日益威胁着国家科技安全，表现最为典型和突出的就是国防科技领域。随着我国改革开放的深入，经济的快速发展以及科技实力的不断增强，大量有价值的科研成果不断涌现。这就必然要求我国加强科技安全工作。当代计算机及其网络技术的日新月异和广泛普及应用，使国家科技安全的问题更加突出，同时引发国家科技保密工作运行方式的变革，保密、窃密的斗争更加呈现高科技抗衡的特点，这使刚刚起步的我国科技保密工作面临着更为严峻的挑战。加强科技安全机制建设，确保国家安全和利益，是国家发展的必然要求。开展这方面的系统研究，具有重要的战略意义。

由于历史的原因，我国在过去相当长一段时间内，科技保密工作没有得到充分的重视，管理体制和措施都已经无法适应新的环境,不能满足当前的需要。随着改革开放的深入,加入世界贸易组织和我国科技实力的不断增强,国家相关管理部门已充分意识到我国科技保密管理方面问题的严重性和紧迫性,正积极进行相关管理体制、制度的建设,努力将制定的一系列科技保密管理制度落到实处。为了制定出有效的、适合当前国际国内环境要求的科技保密管理制度落实的措施,迫切需要对国际上最先进的科技保密机制有充分的了解,以期站在前人的肩膀上,迅速有效地建立起我国的科技保密管理机制。可见,开展国防科技保密机制研究具有重大的现实意义。

本书分析国防科技安全的管理需求,对西方先进国家国防科技保密机制的发展趋势做出归纳和比较,在此基础上对美国的国防科技安全机制作了系统剖析和评价,深入探讨了国防科技保密机制的核心问题和争论焦点,得出对建设和完善我国的国防科技保密机制有益的国际经验与启示。

目 录

第一章 引 言 …………………………………………（1）

第一节 研究背景和目的……………………………（1）
第二节 研究范围和方法……………………………（4）

第二章 国防保密需求的产生 ………………………（7）

第一节 国防科技发展与科技转移政策的发展………（7）
第二节 国防科技保密客体的界定……………………（9）
第三节 科技研发过程的保密需求……………………（11）
第四节 技术转移过程的保密需求……………………（13）

第三章 国防科技保密机制的国际趋势 ……………（16）

第一节 国防科技研发与技术转移政策的发展………（16）
　一、国家机密保护立法……………………………（16）
　二、国内科技研发信息保密立法…………………（19）
　三、国际科学技术保密立法………………………（23）
　四、商业秘密保护立法……………………………（27）

第二节　保密与推广应用并重的做法与成效……………（29）
　　一、美国国防技术转移与保密协调的做法与成效
　　　………………………………………………………（29）
　　二、我国国防技术转移与保密协调的做法与成效
　　　………………………………………………………（30）

第四章　美国国防科技保密的机制……………………（32）

第一节　国家机密保护机制………………………………（32）
　　一、美国政府的国家机密保护机制……………………（32）
　　二、敏感性但非属机密信息的保密做法………………（34）
　　三、白宫在9·11事件后的新政策………………………（35）
第二节　国内科技保密法…………………………………（37）
　　一、发明秘密法…………………………………………（37）
　　二、技术转移过程的科技保密…………………………（40）
　　三、其他有关法案………………………………………（42）
第三节　国际科技保密制度………………………………（44）
　　一、美国主导国际间科技出口管制……………………（44）
　　二、美国政府的科技出口管制…………………………（45）
第四节　商业秘密法………………………………………（47）
　　一、美国商业秘密法……………………………………（48）
　　二、美国经济间谍法案…………………………………（50）
第五节　国防科技保密规范………………………………（52）
　　一、国防部信息安全计划………………………………（52）
　　二、国家产业安全计划作业手册………………………（54）
　　三、《国防部对研究及技术保护的规定程序》草案
　　　………………………………………………………（55）
第六节　美国国防科技保密机制简评……………………（56）

第五章　国防科技保密机制建设争议与问题 (58)

第一节　美国政府实施科技保密的法制争议 (58)
一、国家机密保护法制的争议 (58)
二、国内科技保密法制的争议 (65)
三、国际科技保密法制的争议 (70)
四、经济间谍法案的争议 (74)

第二节　科技保密法制面临的两难困境 (77)
一、信息保密 vs. 科技创新 (77)
二、权威行政 vs. 私权保护 (82)
三、保密管制 vs. 言论自由 (88)
四、国家机密保护 vs. 政府信息公开 (92)

第三节　科技保密法制 (97)
一、科技研发成果的定义 (98)
二、秘密种类的分析及国防科技秘密定义探讨 (102)

第六章　启　示 (108)

参考文献 (111)

附录1　法案、专有名词中英文对照表 (115)

附录2　美国《拜杜法案》(Bayh – Dole Act, 1980) (121)

第一章

引 言

第一节 研究背景和目的

第二次世界大战以后,新的一次技术革命在世界范围内悄然兴起,它以前所未有的速度推动着社会生产力的发展。进入 20 世纪 80 年代,科学技术发展更为迅速,科技进步推动经济和社会发展的作用愈加显著,科技已经渗透到了经济、政治、军事以及社会生活的各个方面。科技实力可以转化成经济动力、军事能力和政治资本,关系到国家的经济振兴、国防巩固和国际地位,对提高综合国力起着十分重要的作用,对国际政治、经济的总格局有着深刻的影响。

进入 21 世纪,科技创新和科技进步不仅推动了社会生产力的迅猛发展和人们生活质量的提高,也对政治、经济、军事活动产生了重大的影响。世界各国竞相把发展科学技术作为捍卫国家利益、确保国家安全、促进经济发展、提高综合国力的关键,使世界范围内的科技竞争日趋激烈。国力的竞争,归根到底是科技实力的竞争。科技安全成了国家安全、乃至人类安全的重要组成部分和技术基础。

在科技竞争中，由于科技窃密活动的特殊作用，它已被视为取得竞争优势的重要手段。随着我国改革开放的深入，经济的快速发展以及科技实力的不断增强，大量有价值的科研成果不断涌现。这就必然要求我国必须开展科技保密工作。

保密、窃密工作是没有硝烟的战场。科技秘密，特别是关系着国家安全与利益的重大国家科技秘密，历来是竞争对手窃取的目标。尤其是计算机及其网络技术的日新月异和广泛普及应用，使国家科技安全的问题更加突出，同时引发国家科技保密工作运行方式的变革，保密、窃密的斗争更加呈现高科技抗衡的特点，这使刚刚起步的我国科技保密工作面临着更为严峻的挑战。

因此，加强科技保密工作，确保国家安全和利益，是新的历史条件下的必然要求。在新的历史条件下，完善我国科技保密体系的建设，提高我国科技保密管理工作的现代化水平，具有重要的战略意义。但是，由于历史的原因，在过去相当长一段时间内，我国科技保密工作没有得到充分的重视，管理体制和措施都已经无法适应新的环境，不能满足当前的需要。随着改革开放的深入，加入世界贸易组织和我国科技实力的不断增强，国家相关管理部门已充分意识到我国科技保密管理方面问题的严重性和紧迫性，正积极进行相关管理体系、制度的建设，努力将制定的一系列科技保密管理制度落到实处。为了制定出有效的、适合当前国际国内环境要求的科技保密管理制度落实措施，就必须对国际上最先进的科技保密体系有充分的了解，以期站在前人的肩膀上，迅速有效地建立起我国的科技保密管理体系。本书将对美国国防科技保密体系作一初步探索，为借鉴和吸收经验，提供基础。

在第二次世界大战中，美国以先进的科技（包括雷达、原子弹技术）和强大的工业基础取得胜利；到冷战时期，进一步突破传统观念，不在武器或士兵数量上与前苏联及华沙公约部队分庭抗礼，而是发展出"抵销战略"，即以技术优势抗衡敌方兵力数量上的优势。这种"抵销战略"有两项组成要素：第一，积极从事军事技术研究开发工作，并发展出拥有高技术含量的国防工业基础；第二，通过技术保密及出口管制保护国防科技机密，阻止敌人获得所需技术。

冷战结束后，美国发现维持技术优势面临着越来越大的挑战。这一挑战主要来自于以往主要是由政府的国防经费建立的，且几乎完全属于国家所有的，支持美国军事优势的工业和技术基础如今已面临"商业化"及"全球化"趋势的冲击。"商业化"趋势是指政府无法再无限制地以政府预算投入国防，对国家安全至为重要的技术渐渐来自商业界，国防工业也趋于市场化；"全球化"的趋势则是指科学技术的特性，以及从事科技研发的公司不论在外观、所有权、人力及市场等方面，都越来越具有全球性的特质。在这种情形下，对核心和关键国防科技实施严格的保密，显得越发重要。

及至9·11恐怖攻击事件发生，美国国家安全遭遇重大冲击，美国政府开始重新全面检讨国家安全的监控管理机制。面对无形的、可能无所不在的恐怖分子威胁，军事科技的保密重要性更加突出，美国政府于是针对科技信息的管制与保密，采取了一连串的措施，包括限制大学从事科技研发信息的公开、禁止部分国际间学术交流活动及严格审查外国学生参与科技研究等，也使世界各国纷纷重新反省如何紧缩管制，使自冷战结束后追求科技信息自由化、国际化并鼓励科技创新的思潮发生改变，国防科技保密的需求受到极大重视。政府基于国家安全，执行军事科技方面的保密或管制措施，很明显产生国家安全利益对于科技发展、个人权利等方面之间的冲突，形成法律上的重大议题，亟需深入探讨。

国防科技保密问题，涉及政府必须以公权力介入科技研究，产生国家安全利益与政府必须促进科技发展、维护个人权利之间的严重冲突，如何在法制上寻求平衡，具有法学探讨上的重要价值与意义。本书即以美国为主要研究对象，比较各国相关法制的发展，探讨我国国防科技研发及技术转移所衍生的机密维护与安全管制问题，并对我国亟待建立的国防科技保密的法制规范进行研究，希望能提出建议并作为政策法规制订的参考。

第二节　研究范围和方法

本书研究主题是针对国防科技保密的法制。狭义的保密是指针对特定人员、特定场所，或在特定系统内，防止信息对外泄漏；传统的国防科技研发工作，是由政府自行出资、设置专门机构进行研发制造，保密的措施多由政府主管部门或机构自行制定及执行，属于狭义的保密制度。但现代化国家的国防科技发展，已必须借重民间科技力量，才能举全国科技实力支持国防建设，因此，广义的国防科技保密是以"国家"为受保护的对象，并非仅针对特定机关或场所，而执行保密的行为主体，则涵盖在国家管辖领土范围内能接触科技研发成果或信息的所有人员及法人，而非仅针对特定系统内的人员。如何制定各种法律制度，形成完整的国家科技保密系统，以防止外国某些人士、国内非法分子、潜伏间谍、恐怖分子等取得科学技术信息，并避免其对整体国家安全造成危害，将有别于传统上针对局部性、封闭性的保密管制做法。

所以，本书研究范围界定为广义的国防科技保密，涵盖政府对于科学技术的"保密"、"管制"或"保护"等各种限制或干涉科技研发及技术转移的制度。而且,所谓"国防科技"与一般性的科学技术,并无明确的界限,任何科学技术成果,都有可能运用在军事用途上,成为国防科技,政府必须运用"保密"、"管制"、"保护"的措施,介入科技研发或技术转移。在维护国家安全目的下,所谓"科技保密"、"科技管制"或"科技保护",仅具有程度上的差异,事实上都是政府限制或干涉科技研发及技术转移的做法。为了以国家安全为最高目的,有关科技"保密"、"管制"或"保护"的法制都是本书的研究范围,因此,所涵盖的文献资料、法令规范等相当广泛,将采用一般的法学研究方法加以整理、分析及比较。包括:

1. 比较法:美国为科技研发最先进国家之一,国防科技研发与技术转移活动也最为发达,因此为本书主要研究对象;同时对于如欧盟、日本等法制先进国家,也就所能收集到的资料作些辅助探讨。

2. 体系分析:国防科技研发与技术转移制度及其保密法制,受到国家安全、科技研发、技术转移、知识产权方面等多种法律体系交互影响。因此,应从不同角度思考,寻求适宜的法制政策设计。

3. 类型化比较:国防科技研发与技术转移,涉及政府实施保密、管制或保护等不同类型的法规与措施,触及不同法律研究主题,因此,从不同类型的立法政策目的、规范性质等加以比较分析。

4. 法律经济分析的观点:法律经济分析,即在于以经济学的方法来分析法律问题,国防投资与经济建设本来就有经济效益的权衡分析问题。本书并非全面采用经济分析的方法来研究问题,而是对于部分法规制度涉及经济效益比较时,将考虑引用法律经济分析的观点探讨问题。

至于本书的论述研究的方法，着重在二阶段论证法，即第一阶段的"形式有效性分析法"及第二阶段的"实质适宜性判断法"。

一、形式有效性分析法

所谓形式有效性分析，是将现行存在的法律规则作为研究分析的客体，并探求这一法律规范的内涵，目的在先确立所欲分析的法律客体，因而在此分析阶段，以法令规章、文献资料的收集整理并进行比较分析为主，尚未介入主观的价值判断，仅涉及对法律秩序现状的客观分析与解释。

本书对国防科技保密的研究，将通过形式有效性分析先了解国内外有关技术转移法制现状，进而由"理论认识"与"法律实践"的角度切入，通过一般规范理论及实务经验的讨论，发掘重大议题进行探讨，再进一步思考政府应如何建立国防科技保密法制规范。

二、实质适宜性判断法

所谓实质适宜性判断，重点在就主观法律秩序做验证的判断工作，目的在对法规形式实践结果判断其所产生的社会功能、效果及其在法律上位价值理念下的适宜性问题。因此，本书将就我国的国家安全与国防科技保密的需求，进行法制的思考及设计，针对科技保密规范及其相关法理作出分析，提出相应的见解。

第二章
国防保密需求的产生

第一节 国防科技发展与科技转移政策的发展

国防科技与国防工业的发展,不仅关系着国家及全体国民生命财产的安全,并且直接影响一个国家的经济实力与政治实力。因此,尽管世界各国战略思想不同,工业及科技水平相差悬殊,但发展国防工业,掌握关键技术,维持及提升军品自制率等,仍是各国共同的做法,尤其是先进国家,无不投入大量的人力及财力,以保持优势地位。

传统上,国防科技研发一向被视为公共部门的事务,通常由国家在政府机关内部设立研究机构,采取封闭性的体系进行研发,以保持秘密性,防止敌人刺探,便于取得作战上的优势。但国家的资源有限,当政府预算大量投入国防建设时,势必排挤其他部门的预算,导致国家整体建设的失衡。因此,现代化的国家除了从经济学上"机会成本"的角度,不断衡量国防预算支出的适当比例外,更进一步地希望能将国防预算从"支出"的性质转化为"投资"的性质，发挥经济效益。尤其在国防科技发展上尤为显著，因为今日已可看到的许多高科技产业，例如半导体、航天、光电材料、无线通讯等，莫不源自于国防科技研发的成果，使国防预算也能在国家经济、民生福祉上产生贡献。所以，妥善规划国防科技发展政策与计划，结合民生科技及产业发展需求，已成为世界各国所努力的目标。其中的重点，就是利用科学技术具有转化、创新的特性，促进政府研究机构与民间部门之间的技术转移；不论是将政府研究成果转移民间进行商品化发展，或是利用民间研发成果开发军事武器，都是国防科技政策必须考虑的重点。

美国与前苏联在冷战时期的军备竞赛，即提供了一个明显见证，冷战时期的结束，并非双方武器系统投入战场直接厮杀的胜负所造成，而是前苏联因为无法兼顾军备与民众消费需求的发展，而造成的严重结果。美国不仅在第二次世界大战后，即重视军用技术的衍生产品开发，以国防促进经济发展；更在冷战结束后，为了维持巨额的国防经费，进一步大力推动军用技术转移及军民两用技术（dual use technology）的开发。因此，自1980年起，陆续通过《拜杜法案》（Bayh-Dole Act, 1980）（The Stevenson-Wydler Technology Innovation Act, 1980）、《联邦技术转移法》（Federal Technology Transfer Act, 1986）、《国防科技转换、转投资及转移协助法案》（Defense Technology Conversion, Reinvestment, Transition and Assistance Act）等法案，推动政府出资（其中国防科技研究占50%以上）委托的研发成果赋予民间使用的权力而加以商品化，并建立技术转移制度，以带动科技产业创新发展，发挥经济效益，使美国在军事上及经济上持续维持世界强权的地位。

所以，重视国防科技发展的国家，已不能忽视政府与民间的科技互动与交流。我国也于20世纪80年代中期大力推动"军转民"

的工作,推动军工技术转化民用,并制定《国防专利条例》(1990)、《科学技术进步法》(1993)、《促进科技成果转化法》(1996)、《国防法》(1997)等法规,大力推动国防科技工业转移民间支持经济建设。

概括起来,国防科技的技术转移,已成为政府从事国防科技研发的重要一环,但是国防技术转移的推动,包括军用技术转出民用(spin–off)、民用技术转入军用(spin–on)和开发军民通用(dual use)的技术,涉及层面广泛而复杂,但最重要的问题是其所衍生的机密维护与安全管制需求。因为,国防科技发展无法限制在政府体系内部进行,技术数据自然容易外流,就可能被敌对国家取得而研究反制的道,或被非法分子运用进行恐怖攻击等,这样反而危害国家安全。所以,国防科技的发展,必须重视保密,以往传统方式是由政府内部单位进行研发,重点在于研发过程的保密,在各国纷纷重视国防科技技术转移以后,更新增了技术转移过程的保密需求。接下来将先从国防科技保密客体的定义问题,及针对国防科技"研发"及"技术转移"两阶段的过程,说明研究国防科技保密法制的需求日益明显。

第二节

国防科技保密客体的界定

国防科技保密法制的探讨,应先定义需要规范的法律行为主体及客体。执行科技保密的主体,包括执行研发人员、拥有研发成果主体、接受技术转移主体、或接触研发信息主体,视保密的范围、强度、目的等因素施加不同程度的保密义务。因此，运用民法上的观念，以能享有权利、负担义务的权利主体，即自然人与法人，作为科技保密法制上的行为主体，是没有疑义的；但在保密客体方面，因为科技研发的特性使然，难以明确定义，尤其是"国防科技"如何定义？国防科技成果或研发信息中需要保密的"机密"或"秘密"是什么？在国防科技发展强调技术转移及借重民间力量的趋势下，就成为探讨国防科技保密法制的基本需求。

所谓"国防"，狭义上，是指军事上的实力配置，军事上的国防设备，即指使用武力的结构或组织及其行动。但广义上，则无论有形的政治、军事、经济、社会、内政、外交、交通、资源及无形的文化、教育等都在这一范围之内。按广义的国防定义，"国防科技"应包括与国家安全有直接、间接相关的科学技术，涵盖基础性、应用性及系统发展各层面的科技研究，这样的范围当然包含了民间从事非国防目的的科学技术研究开发，在其研究成果或信息中，有可能被应用于国防建设上，或可能对国家安全产生影响的，都属于国防科技的范围。例如，我国一般称为"军民通用科技"或"军民两用技术"等，都因可能有军事运用的可能性，因此符合本书的国防科技范围。但科学技术成果常以无形的知识（know－how）形态存在，通常难以描述或定义，包括我国的科学技术法都未对科技有所定义，因此，采用广义的国防科技的范围定义基本上具有不确定法律概念的性质，且其认定标准甚难界定，若要再进一步将其界定为需要保密的范围，更有值得深入研究探讨的必要。

至于我国法律上对于需要保密的客体，多称为"机密"或"秘密"。不论是"国家机密"或"国防秘密"，都是指政府机关内部所产生或持有的保密信息，并无法涵盖全民国防概念中可能由民间所自行研发的科技的保密需求；而"商业秘密"的定义中，则未能突显与国防建设或国家安全有关的科技信息的保密需求。因此，如何对国防科技保密客体的定义和范围做出明确的界定，随着国防科技发展具有全球化、商业化及转移民间的趋势，将更加复杂及困难，产生了对国防科技保密法制作为主题进行探讨的需求。

第三节

科技研发过程的保密需求

人类科技能不断地进步，在于研究发明成果的累积、突破，进而产生创新，所以，知识心得的交流和思想创意的沟通是促进科技进步的重要因素。一般而言，闭门造车式的科技研发系统，缺乏有效的省察机制，沟通交流机制不良，在研究发现程序上不具有竞争力。但是研发过程中仍免不了有保密的需要，例如，避免研发过程被干扰、防止竞争对手模仿、保护商业利益等因素，会促使研发者自主性地采取保密措施；至于由政府介入，强制研发人员保密的，则多基于国家安全、公共利益等因素。

由于军事科技的发展攸关国家安全，政府必然有保密管制上的需求考虑。首先，政府所资助的研究开发，其计划背景就可能涉及国防需要，自然必须保密，以维持战略或战术上的价值；其次，民间自行从事的研发活动，因研发成果也可能具有军事上的运用价值，或可能对国家安全产生危害，因此政府也有介入要求保密的必要。所以，对于一个从事国防科技研发人员而言，往往必须在两个法制系统间寻求调和，即国家的"科技发展"和"情报管理"法制。因为，国家制定科技发展政策及法制，应该鼓励科学技术知识的流通；而国家执行情报管理工作，则必须对信息的流动和可以知悉的人员加以限制，所以，从事国防科技研发的工作者，必须有适当的安全认知，才能对所接触的知识或信息，作妥善处理，并恰如其分尽其应有的社会责任。

介于鼓励科技信息自由流通与执行保密限制之间的，是知识产权法制。知识产权制度的产生，是一个符合人性的设计，利用赋予创作人拥有财产权的法律诱因，促进科技研究成果的披露和持续创新发明；整个制度最重要的部分，在于创作人的财产权与公共利益的调和。但知识产权法除了对研究成果予以保护外，对于研究成果形成之前，即研究过程中所搜集的信息，及产出的初步概念，包括一些调查数据、实验数据，甚或失败经验等，是否予以保护？这也是知识产权制度上容有争议之处。所以，在传统的专利权、著作权及商标权外，引起知识产权学界重视，产业界也乐于实施的是"商业秘密"的制度。商业秘密法制就是一种科技保密的制度，从研发过程的纵向面及横向面的保密需求，都可以加以涵盖，只要标的物符合一定的要件、拥有者善尽保密的作为，即可赋予法律上的权利加以保护。

商业秘密的制度证明科技研发过程确有保密需求。而国防科技研发一向都是针对最尖端、最前瞻的科技，通常需要投入巨额的研发经费及庞大人力等资源，却负有极高的风险性，更有保密及安全维护上的需求，其研发成果非常需要由知识产权观点和政府建立保密机制来加以管理及保护。随着国家、社会不断进步，国防科技保密需求更为殷切，主要有以下原因：

1. 如同前文所述的国防科技政策的演变，民间参与国防科技研发活动越来越频繁和深入，已无法在政府内部进行封闭式的研发。

2. 科技的进展使信息取得容易，如因特网、卫星通信的技术，

第二章 国防保密需求的产生

已使信息的交流和沟通无远弗界。

3. 科技信息的特性常使人难以辨别其保密需求。有些是基础性的学术研究信息，应该是要鼓励披露及交流使用才对；有些是应用性的科技成果，却无法完全了解其用途，因此，非有同时具备该技术领域专门知识及了解国家安全需求的人，无法轻易作成是否需要保密的判断。而这些原因及背景，即突显出政府建立国防科技保密制度的迫切性及复杂性。

第四节

技术转移过程的保密需求

现代化国家莫不重视科学技术的研究开发，以达成国防、经济、民生、社会的重大进步。而科技研究开发的成果，必须经历技术转移、技术扩散的阶段，才能直接为一般民众所享用。因此，政府投入预算进行科技研究，若未能同时建立技术转移及技术扩散的机制，将技术成果商品化以造福民生，或产业化以促进经济成长，则这一科技政策将无法发挥综合效果（synergy）。因此，科技发展过程中"技术转移"扮演着桥梁的功能，是科技发展成功与否的关键性因素。因此，现代化先进国家政府均积极建立技术转移制度，并将其视为科技政策、产业政策、国防政策的一环。

美国在过去冷战时期基于国家安全的优先性及传统科研环境、文化影响，也倾向保持技术的封闭性。但在克林顿政府时期，通过国会的支持，在相关执行措施上有很大突破。克林顿就职一个月后即提出报告指出："行政部门将修正方法，在互利的情况下促进联邦机构与民间产业的合作……"在技术发展层次，实现政府与民间产业合作的基础机制，就是通过合作研发来分摊研发成本。政府将鼓励所有联邦研究机构（包含所属实验室）"尽可能地扮演产业界的伙伴角色，使政府预算投入能同时满足政府需要和社会经济发展需求。政府机构将优先排除执行合作研发合约（CRADAs）的障碍，并利用其他方式促进产研合作"。

美国为了促使国防科技成果能转移民间，克林顿政府时期即专门针对国防科技方面的成果转移及利用，由国防部设立技术转移办公室，并颁布了相关法案，结合能源部（DOE）、商务部（DOC）、国家标准技术院（NIST）、国家科学基金会（NSD）、国家航空太空总署（NASA）等科技研究单位，由国防部先进研究计划局（DARPA）主导，从事"技术转移投资项目计划"（Technology Reinvestment Program，TRP）的推动工作，国防部并制定国内技术转移政策，要求国防部单位及所属研究机构执行。相同的，我国在《国防法》中也强调"国防科技工业实行军民结合、平战结合、军品优先、以民养军的方针"，国务院也颁布《关于加强军工科研院所与企业结合进一步促进军转民工作若干意见》等政策指示。而政府执行国防科技技术转移工作，增加了安全控管上的风险，也可以从以下几个角度了解到技术转移过程中的科技保密需求大为增加。

1. 执行技术转移工作，难免地增加了国防科技信息外泄的渠道，政府研究机构将科技研发成果转移民间时，通常必须同时交付相关的技术数据、文件、手册，可能将当初的设计理念、应用范围等敏感信息暴露出来，加上转手数据的研发、管理人员增加，因其过失或疏忽而致泄密的可能性也升高。

2. 经济上的诱因也会使接受技转的单位或人员忽视国防安全，这是因为政府的技术转移制度，一向鼓励民间将政府研发成果进行商品化发展，而基于商业利益，获得技转的单位或人员，将不会主动考虑后续商品化的应用是否不利于国家安全，或甚至蒙蔽政府机关，对国家社会造成危害。

3. 政府推动技术转移政策，必须遵守信息公开的法制，必然在安全控管上产生风险，包括一些尖端科技信息被有心人士取得，或是政府研究方向被敌人知悉等。所以，一个国家推动国防科技技术转移成功的关键因素之一，就在于其搭配的安全保密制度是否健全，也说明了国防科技保密的重要性。

第三章
国防科技保密机制的国际趋势

第一节
国防科技研发与技术转移政策的发展

本书对美、英、德、日等国家的政策法制进行收集比较,这些国家均非常重视科技发展在未来军事作战中的关键性地位,因此都积极支持国防科技发展,并且产生国防科技保密的需求。经过比较观察可以发现,这些国家的国防科技保密有相同之处,即国防科技保密无法单纯地以制定单一的特别法就能达成,经过整理,可以区分出政府是利用国家机密保护、国内科学技术保密、国际科学技术保密及商业秘密保护等四种不同法律系统,来建构完整的国防科技保密制度,保障国家安全。其中美国的法制是本书主要深入研究的对象,将在下一章中以专章探讨。

一、国家机密保护立法

国家机密的保护,自有政府或国家体制以来,即依附在国家安全与秩序维护的功能下。即使近来自由民主意识抬头，在政府信息公开的法制潮流下，对所谓"国家机密"，仍能在法制规范形式面上受到充分保护。这是因为"国家机密"的定义或实质、内涵，常隐晦不明，但在公民权、阳光政府及人民知情权意识升高后，民众对于何谓"国家机密"，就有要求立法说明清楚的强烈诉求。所以，发达国家都至少在形式上将"国家机密"以法律明确规范，或明确规定"国家机密"的内容与管理方式，使与一般阳光法律有清楚的界限。

（一）美、英、德、日等国家的国家机密保护

美国是利用总统的行政命令建立国家机密的分类等级及相关保密规定。同样的，如德、英、日等国家也都以法律或政府的行政规定建立国家机密保护的机制。德国有《联邦安全检查法》，规定政府机关中从事与安全事务有关的人员或被委托安全事务的人被检查时的要件及其程序。依德国《联邦安全检查法》第四条，即对政府的"秘密事项"（Verschluβ sahen）定义为："指在国家利益上具有保密需要且独立于其陈述方式的事实、对象或见解"，并且将秘密事项分级为"绝对机密"（STRENG GEHEIM）、"极机密"（GEHEIM）、"机密"（VS – VERTRAULICH）、"秘密"（VS – NUR FÜR DEN DIENSTGEBRAUCH）四级。且德国依据《联邦安全检查法》第三十五条第一项及《基本法》第八十六条的规定，制定秘密事项保护的一般行政规定，对于可能影响国家安全的信息加以保密及保护。

英国于1911年即制定《公务机密法》，并于1920年、1939年、1980年数度增修，规范与国家安全、情报有关对象或信息的保密与保护方式。

日本对于行政机关机密的保护，是由昭和四十年的事务次官等会议决议的《关于机密文书等的处理》办理，规定机密文书区分为

"极秘"、"秘密"两个等级,"极秘"是指机密保护的必要较高,泄漏有损及国家安全及利益之虞;而"秘密"级的程度是指不宜使关系以外的人知悉。昭和四十七年则进一步制定《国家机密各种机密的基准》,对"关于外交、国际经济、防卫"、"有关个人的秘密"、"基于职务的特殊性"、"一定期间内有保密的必要"等四种内阁官房执行保密的信息,提出例示规定,其"一定期间内有保密的必要"即例示"专利申请文件",如不保密有使申请专利的人蒙受不测损害之虞,则政府机关应采取保密措施。前文规定是以行政命令的方式颁布,由行政机关遵守执行的,但因日本与美国有共同防卫的协议,因此,为了维护两国在军事合作方面的机密事项,曾以法律颁布《伴随日美防卫援助协议的秘密保护法》界定"特别防卫秘密"的名称与相关规定,以达到保密要求。

这些国家的国家机密信息中,通过实质的认定,基本上都涵盖了由政府所持有或保管的国防科技机密成果及信息,但除美国外,并未在法律条文形式上明确指出科学技术方面的信息属于国家机密信息的一类。

(二)我国的《保守国家秘密法》

我国保护国家机密的法制,是以《中华人民共和国保守国家秘密法》(以下简称《保守国家秘密法》)为基本法。该法是于1988年9月5日经第七届全国人民代表大会常务委员会第三次会议通过,自1989年5月1日起施行,这是我国继1951年《保守国家机密暂行条例》后,关于保守国家秘密工作的一部重要立法。

早在1951年即由周恩来总理签署并公布施行《保守国家机密暂行条例》,其后30余年,该条例均为我国执行国家机密安全维护工作的准则。但从20世纪80年代起,我国实行改革开放,为了确保国家秘密并有利于改革开放,进而保障和促进社会主义建设事业的顺利进行,产生了《保守国家秘密法》的立法需求。在该法通过

第三章　国防科技保密机制的国际趋势

的同时，人大常委会还通过了《关于惩治泄露国家秘密犯罪的补充规定》，作为相关配套措施，从而建立起我国的国家机密保护法制。

依我国《保守国家秘密法》第八条所规定的保密范围中，第五款明确指出"科学技术中的秘密事项"，此外第十九条规定："属于国家秘密的设备或者产品的研制、生产、运输、使用、保存、维修和销毁，由国家保密工作部门会同中央有关机关制定保密办法。"可以看出在我国的国家机密保护体系中，相当重视科学技术方面的保密需求。另外该法在第三十四条规定："中央军事委员会根据本法制定中国人民解放军保密条例。"作为军方再进一步建立保密体系的法律授权依据。

二、国内科技研发信息保密立法

（一）美、英、德、法、日等国家的专利保密

美国政府针对科技研发活动，采取多种渠道执行科技研发成果的相关信息保密与限制公开，其中最具代表性的法制应属专利保密制度，其他国家也有类似的立法例。德国专利法第五十条即专利保密的规定，对已经申请专利的发明是国家机密时，审查处依职权应命令不作任何公告。在命令前，应听取负权责的联邦最高机关的意见。德国专利法第五十二条规定在德意志联邦共和国外申请专利，需经负权责的联邦最高机关给与书面同意后，才得在本法的适用范围外提起含有国家机密的专利申请；第五十四条则规定，对于依据第五十条第一项规定的命令申请授予专利时，应在特别的登记簿内登记专利。

英国专利法第二十二条规定，当一件专利申请案向专利局提出，而专利局局长认为该申请案在其说明中包含有国务大臣提请他注意的内容，其发表可能危害国防安全的情报时，专利局局长即可发出指示，禁止或限制该项情报的发表或向某些人传告。而且：

(1) 如果申请案是按本法提出的，它可进行到这样一个阶段，即：该件申请案已经准备好只待批准专利，但是它不应被发表，有关的情报不应传告，也不应根据申请案授予专利；(2) 假如是一件欧洲专利申请，不得送到欧洲专利局；(3) 如果是国际专利申请，该申请案的抄本不应被送往国际专利局，或送往专利合作条约委托的任何国际查文件单位。该条文对于保密的做法有详细的规定。

法国发明专利法第二十四条规定国防部长有权向全国工业产权局，完全对外保密地了解专利申请情况。负责工业产权的部长，可根据国防部长的意见，下令不得随意泄露或实施。第四十条规定国家因国防需要，随时可颁发许可证征用作为专利或专利申请案的发明，不论是国家本身，或是由国家付款实施此发明。第四十五条更规定国家为了国防需要可随时依据负责工业产权的部长和国防部长的报告制定法令，全部或部分地征用申请专利或已批专利的发明。

日本则在发明（特许）专利法第一百八十六条规定，有关专利证明的申请，任何人都可以向特许厅长官申请有关发明专利的证明、文件资料的副本或抄本，也可申请阅览或复写文件数据或发明专利权中利用磁带制作的文件数据。但特许厅长官认为有保持秘密的必要的，不受这个规定的限制。

（二）我国的国防专利制度

各国对涉及国家安全或重大利益者均会采取保密措施，其做法基本上有两种形式：一是将发明创造保密，在解密前不授予专利权，例如美国、法国、英国、希腊等国；二是将发明创造专利申请保密，经过审查合格的授予专利权，但不进行公布，例如意大利、土耳其、比利时、荷兰、挪威等国。鉴于后者既达到保密目的，又可以在控制下推广应用，因此，我国秘密专利原则上是采用后者。但规定对列为绝密级的国防秘密，仍不得申请专利。

我国第一部《中华人民共和国专利法》（以下简称《专利法》）

第三章 国防科技保密机制的国际趋势

于 1985 年 4 月 1 日正式施行，其中第四条规定："申请专利的发明创造涉及国家安全或者重大利益需要保密的，按照国家有关规定办理。"国防科学技术工业委员会（以下简称"国防科工委"）于 1987 年成立国防专利局，作为国防专利申请的专责机构，1990 年国务院、中央军事委员会（以下简称"中央军委"）正式批准颁布《国防专利条例》。

整体来说，我国国防专利制度实际包含两个层次：首先就是以《国防专利条例》为特别法，作为申请和审批国防专利法律依据；其次，包括我国《专利法》、《中华人民共和国专利法实施细则》（以下简称《专利法实施细则》），及依保密的要求而涉及的国家秘密的规定，如《保守国家秘密法》、《保守国家秘密法实施办法》、科学技术保密规定及国防科学技术成果国家秘密的保密和解密办法等几个重要的保密法规等，都与国防专利的运作管理有关联性。

1. 我国的国防专利定义。国防专利是指涉及国防利益以及对国防建设有潜在作用需要保密的发明专利。

国防专利与普通专利的主要区别在于：国防专利只在国防系统内公开摘要，不公开具体的说明书；而普通专利则向全世界之公众全面公开，任何人均可以查阅说明书及权利要求书等文档；国防专利采用实时审查制，审查速度比普通专利快。此外，国防专利还设有补偿费，可以补偿国防专利权人因保密而造成的一部分损失。对于拟申请国防专利的技术，还应请国防专利代理机构办理。

2. 我国国防专利的范围及保密程序。我国《国防专利条例》是依《专利法》第四条授权制定的，由其条文所称："申请专利的发明创造涉及国家安全或者重大利益需要保密的，按照国家有关规定办理"，此处的"发明创造"范围虽包含发明、实用新型及外观设计，但从实践来看，外观设计一般与国家安全或重大利益关系不大，而且一旦应用到工业品上，在市场上销售，就无密可保，实用新型的创造性水平较低，影响到国家安全或者重大利益的可能性也不大，因此，本条所指的发明创造，实际上主要是指发明，纳入国防专利，均应属发明专利。此外，依《国防专利条例》第四条第一项规定，绝密级涉及国防利益的发明不得申请国防专利，因此，国防专利范围着重在既可用于国防又可民用的发明创造，以后根据需要，可以按照有关规定进行解密，转为普通专利。所以，国防专利并非以保密为最主要考虑，而是以管理及运用为目的。

关于保密程序，还必须先明确"保密专利"与"国防专利"的区别。我国《专利法》第四条对于申请专利需要保密的，包括涉及"国家安全"或者"重大利益"，因此，专利申请需要保密的案件，并非只有国防专利，还包括涉及国家重大利益的一般秘密专利。

国防专利，若由国防系统提出，应向国防专利局申请，专利局应根国防专利局的审查意见作出决定；非国防系统的申请，根据我国《专利法实施细则》第八条第一款的规定，专利局受理的涉及国防方面的国家秘密需要保密的发明专利申请，应当移交国防专利局审查，专利局应根据国防专利局的审查意见作出决定。

一般秘密专利，根据我国《专利法实施细则》第八条第二款的规定，专利局受理发明专利申请后，应当将需要进行保密审查的申请转送国务院有关主管部门审查，有关部门应在收到日起 4 个月内，将审查结果通知专利局。申请专利的发明创造需要保密的，专利局按保密专利处理，并通知申请人。

保密需求的提出，分为：（1）由申请人提出；（2）由专利局提出；（3）国防专利局派人至专利局挑选等三种方式。所以，我国不仅设有国防专利局专责管理国防专利，还可以定期派人到专利局查看普通专利申请，发现其中有涉及国防利益或者对国防建设有潜在作用需要保密的专利申请案,在取得专利局同意后抽出转为国防专利申请,并通知申请人。从科技研发成果保密的角度看,这些研发信息并非直接纳入国家机密,而是以国防专利作保密管理对象,这种做法以国家利益为出发点,管理也更加严谨。

三、国际科学技术保密立法

以国家为主体,除了在国内实施科技研发信息保密,诸如秘密专利等制度外;也有些科技信息是已经在国内公开,但在科技成果运用方面,必须防范有敌意的国家取得,而使国家安全受到危害,或区域及世界和平遭到破坏,因此,国际间对科学技术转移出口进行管制,签订条约共同遵守并落实到国内法中执行,形成国际间的科学技术保密机制。

(一)国际间科技转移的出口管制

出口管制是一个国家基于政治、军事、经济、社会或道德上的义务,禁止或限制该国的产品或其海外的公司所制造的产品,出口至禁止或限制的地区。传统的出口管制,多指有形的货物商品,无形的技术转移较为少见;但随着科学技术发展,技术能力已成为国家经济实力及竞争优势的基础,因此,不论国际间或国家的出口管制,都已将技术项目列为管制对象。

国际间的出口管制,除了有敌意的国家之间是基于政治、军事或政治目的具有制裁性质的禁止出口之外,都必须有国际协议或条约作基础,才能让参与国家共同遵守。目前国际上对于科学技术的出口进行管制,主要以瓦圣那协议及联合国禁止化学武器公约两项为代表。

1. 瓦圣那协议。二次世界大战以后,东西方冷战兴起,西方国家在美国的大力主导之下,为防止具战略性价值的高科技产品和技术流入冷战对手之手,建立了一套管制机制,而为了执行这套管制机制，以美国为首于 1949 年成立了"多边出口管制协调委员会"（Coordinating Committee for Multilateral Export Control，简称 COCOM）。希望借着会员国之间的密切联系，可以有效防止西方国家的高科技流入前苏联集团成员的手中。

之后，前苏联和东欧解体，导致因冷战而设立的高科技出口管制也面临了全面检讨的局面。在 1994 年 3 月 31 日召开最后一次会议后，COCOM 组织正式解散。继于 1995 年 12 月，美、日等 33 个国家成立瓦圣那协议（The Wassenaar Arrangement，简称 WA）取代 COCOM。负责传统武器及军民两用货品的输出管制，配合导弹技术管制协议（MTCR）、核武器国集团（NSG）及澳洲集团（AG）等防止扩散组织，共同防止大规模杀伤性武器的扩散，形成全球安全出口管制制度。

瓦圣那协议能从一个具有军事目的的国际协约转型成一般国家都接受的国际协议，主要是基于该协议促成区域与国际的安全及稳定的宗旨，并凭借着加强信息透明化与责任感、对于军民两用货品与技术转移的管制有明确的清单、以及参与国定期聚会及定期检讨协议的功能等方式取得各国的承认和遵守；且该协议不会用以对抗任何国家，以及不会阻碍善意的（bona fide）民事交易。因此，瓦圣那协议可以说有其理想性，在防止军备及基于军事最终用途的敏感性货品与技术的管制方面，也确实发挥了一定效果。

2. 联合国禁止化学武器公约。联合国禁止化学武器公约是联合国于 1992 年 9 月在日内瓦裁军会议签署公约草案后，同年 11 月第 47 届联合国大会通过，成为公约；1993 年 1 月在法国举行公开签署仪式，接受联合国会员国的签署，2 月于荷兰海牙设立执行机构 OPCW（the Organization for the Prohibition of Chemical Weapons）。依公约的规定，签署达 65 国后的 180 天，该公约正式生效。1996 年

10月匈牙利成为第 65 个缔约国，公约也于 1997 年 4 月 29 日正式生效。1997 年 5 月于海牙举行第一次缔约国大会，各缔约国须完成国内相关立法，遵守公约条文的约束，成立专责机构，申报各项资料，并接受 OPCW 的监督、裁察。其管制的项目以可能生产化学武器的化学制剂为主，当然对其技术也产生管制效果。

其他国家的科技出口管制，均与美国类似，一方面遵守国际间的协约；另一方面将出口管制规范落实于本国的法令中。

（二）欧盟与美国、日本等国家的科技出口管制

欧盟与美国、日本等科技先进国家，基于国家安全利益，特别重视国际间的高科技出口管制制度，除了主导并遵守国际条约外，并且都在其国内法中积极落实执行。

以欧盟为例，有关军民两用高科技货品的出口管制，主要是适用 2000/1334/EC 规则、2000/2998/EC 规则及 2001/458/EC 规则，其是依循瓦圣那协议等国际公约所制定。相较于旧法 94/942/EC 规则，现行法对于欧盟境内管制货品流通已趋自由化，也简化其他需经出口许可的相关程序。因此，除了部分具高度敏感性或特殊性产品（例如解密技术 cryptanalysis items）外，欧盟境内原则上已无管制货品或技术，均可以自由流通。凡列为敏感性或特殊性产品，仅需出具相关文件、声明该产品最终使用、取得欧盟境内一般性许可（General Intra – Community Licenses），即可出口至欧盟境内其他国家。

个别国家也会制定国内法管制技术出口，例如，德国是由经济科技部（Bundesministerium fuer Wirtschaft und Technologie）下的联邦经济及出口管制局（Bundesamt fuer Wirtschaft und Ausfuhrkontrolle）主管高科技出口管制。德国管制技术出口的主要法令规范为《国际贸易法》（Aussenwirtschaftsgesetz）、《国际贸易规则》（Aussenwirtschaftsverordnung）及欧盟 2000/1334/EC 规

则。规范重点包括：(1) 有关武器军备及军民两用货品输出入管制事宜，负责审查出口货品或技术是否需取得出口许可、决定及核发出口许可；(2) 就国际贸易所涉及的调查、刑事程序，提出专业意见；(3) 出口证明申请的可驳；(4) 负责与欧盟出口管理主管机构的联系事宜。此外，德国有《武器管理法》（Kriegswaffenkontrollgesetz），负责监督战争武器生产、运输及出售事宜；而依据生物武器管制国际公约也定有《生物武器出口管理法》（Ausfuehrungsgesetz zum Chemiewaffenuebereinkommen），负责落实生物武器管制、搜集生化工业发展相关资料等。

日本也是瓦圣那协议等国际组织的会员国，因此，也遵守国际公约进行科技出口管制。主要是由经济产业省依据法令审查出口签证申请，受管制物品包括：(1) 瓦圣那协议的管制清单上的武器及组件；(2) 大规模杀伤性武器相关物品；(3) 瓦圣那协议的军民两用管制清单的传统武器相关物品；(4) 与NSG、AG 及 MTCR 等出口管制体系下的管制物品相同类别的物品。而日本管制科技相关货品或技术出口的法律基础，主要是《外汇暨外贸法》（Foreign Exchange and Foreign Trade Law），以及经济产业省据此制定的《出口贸易管理规则》（Export Trade Control Regulation）。厂商在出口货品之前，应先确认该货品是否属于《出口贸易管理规则》所列的管制货品。且依据《外汇暨外贸法》，主管机关在必要时，应在营业时间内，派遣人员进入从事外汇的金融机构或营业商的营业所、事务所或工厂，针对外汇账簿及其他对象，询问相关当事人。因此，日本政府对于可能违法输出货品的公司及个人，要进行必要的检查，此间搜集的资料也可作为日后起诉犯罪的参考。

（三）我国的科技出口管制

我国的出口管制法律架构历经两个时期。1990 年以前，出口管制的法律基础大都是由国务院下相关部门发布的规定；1990年以后则由国务院制定一些行政法规，将出口管制管理法制化。其中1994年颁布《中华人民共和国对外贸易法》，作为规范国际贸易的基本法，其中规定得在特定情况下对进出口加以限制或禁止。而1996年1月发布《中华人民共和国管制化学品管理办法》、1997年9月发布《中华人民共和国核子出口管制办法》、1997年10月发布《中华人民共和国核子双重用途物品及相关技术出口管制办法》，以及在2002年10月14日公布并自12月1日起施行《中华人民共和国生物两用品及相关设备和技术出口管制条例》等，这些陆续发布的法令，都是按照国际间对高科技及大规模破坏武器的管制公约研究制定和执行的。

四、商业秘密保护立法

在知识产权法律体系中，一般都是要求科学技术成果的发明人或拥有人将技术内容公开，而由政府赋予其财产权利，以便于运用公权力保护，但"商业秘密"法制则为例外。为了保护更大的经济利益，"商业秘密"法制允许科技研发信息保持秘密，使得民间产业界愿意自发性地采取保密行为。业界对于研究开发成果选择使用专利或商业秘密来保护研发成果，取决于许多因素，包括产品具有竞争优势的生命周期、使用商业秘密保护的成本与风险、证明专利侵权的困难性、竞争者模仿的困难程度等。例如，竞争者只要购买产品再以逆向工程就可以轻易仿制的技术，应申请专利保护较有利；若是技术内容披露后要证明专利侵权较困难的（如制造方法专利），则应考虑以商业秘密保护。这种业界所普遍熟悉，且愿意自发性采取的保密行为，显然是政府针对"科技保密"可以利用的方法。

以商业秘密法制来保护科技研发成果，已是一种国际趋势。随着经济发展与科技进步，许多国家均认识到传统的知识产权的范畴已经无法应对日新月异的发展，于是逐渐承认其他知识产权类型，例如，软件专利、微生物专利、集成电路布局、商业秘密等。此种对人类研究创作成果扩大保护的趋势，已为世界贸易组织（WTO）所肯定，并由各国签署《与贸易相关的知识产权协议》（TRIPs），成为国际间共同规范。而在这些新兴知识产权中，其重要性及观念创新程度最大的，当属"商业秘密"，这是因为商业秘密的保护不仅可以补充其他知识产权的不足，并可在尚未取得知识产权之前（如研发或实验室阶段），有效地保护创作人权益，并可在结合经营信息保密、防止不公平竞争与规范竞争秩序方面，发挥其特殊的地位，因此，也造成欧盟与美、日等先进国家纷纷以法律对商业秘密加以保护的趋势。

各国对于商业秘密保护的法律，有的是普通法国家以判例形成商业秘密保护要件与规范，如英国；有的国家是以不正当竞争法体系来规范，如德国、日本、韩国等，由于有前文 WTO 的国际条约，因此，各国对于商业秘密的定义与保护方式尚属大同小异，本书中将不再针对个别国家进行介绍。

值得一提的是，有些国家采取制定专法保护商业秘密，例如，美国在州法与判例法之外还由联邦政府制定经济间谍法案等。至于基于国家安全因素，政府直接运用商业秘密法制介入科技成果信息保护者，仅有美国经济间谍法案。但我们也可以发现，如德、日等法制先进国家，对于商业秘密的规范从民法层次提升到不正当竞争法体系中，以政府维护公平交易秩序为目的；换句话说，对商业秘密的违反，已不再是纯粹民事侵权行为，而是有公权力必须介入的需求。由此看来，国家的国防科技保密机制，结合商业秘密法制，由政府提供行政与司法资源，在国家机密范围之外，广泛对科技研发成果加以保护，具有发展的可行性与法制思考上的重大意义。

第三章 国防科技保密机制的国际趋势

第二节

保密与推广应用并重的做法与成效

从以上各国的立法例中,除了了解国防科技保密必须采用多重法制系统的趋势外,还必须注意另一个重点,即国防科技保密并非以保密效果最严密、保密行政成本最低作为考虑,采取封闭式体系从事国防科技研发。现代国家投入政府预算从事科技研发的趋势,是必须能兼顾国家安全、经济效益及科技进步等多重目的,因此,国防预算也必须配合国家整体利益,将国防科技研发委托民间执行,并推动民间产业将这些研发成果商业化,以取得更高的投资效益。这使得先进国家愿意耗费较大的行政成本,运用国家机密保护、科技保密、技术出口管制、商业秘密管理等繁复的法令系统,来达到国防科技保密的目的。

所以,国家建立国防科技保密法制的重要思考之一,不应只以"保密"为主要考虑因素,而应以服务国防科技研发及技术转移为目的。否则,只追求保密而限制科技信息的交流、妨碍政府科技成果流向民间,无异因噎废食、本末倒置。以下以美国及我国为例,说明国防科技保密是必须配合技术转移工作相辅相成地推动。

一、美国国防技术转移与保密协调的做法与成效

美国国防部长依法设置"技术转移办公室"(Office of Technology Transition)的组织,进行军用技术的技术转移研究,筛选及监管国防科技转为民用,使保密与推广能同时并重。该室2002年向国会

提出的报告中,即指出主要任务是提供政策指导、监督及支持军方技术转移,因此,必须整合及确认技术转移项目、参与联邦政府部门与国外技术转移活动的审查等,这都属于政府技转制度中确保国家安全的一环,但最终目的仍在于整合国防科技引进民间部门,增进科技发展和产业基础,所以,就其管理的国防部军民通用科技研发计划(Dual Use S&T Program)为例,在 2001 年就有约 400 个民间企业、学校和非营利性组织参与,执行 327 项计划,总金额超过 10 亿美元。

再如,美国国防部国防科技信息中心(Defense Technology Information Center)也建置数据库及网络系统,就国防科技成果进行分类管理,其 2001 年的统计中,属于公开性的技术报告资料,有 5 452 548 人次上网查询;但属于限制性的数据,则必须登录为会员才能查询及下载,在 2001 年有 5 202 名登录会员、157 955 人次查询,并藉此可以分析这些登录会员的组成及限制性数据的流向。由此可见,国防科技保密管制的重点在于"有效管理",而非一味地隐藏或遮掩。

二、我国国防技术转移与保密协调的做法与成效

我国从 1980 年左右推动"军转民"的工作,并逐步建立完整的国防科技转移民间的推动体制,"国防专利"制度就是其中的一环,以配合国防科研成果转化工作。因此,我国军方所设的国防专利局,每周一次到国家知识产权局对受理的发明专利申请进行查阅,就是要进行保密筛选,将需要保密的专利申请案转由国防专利局受理,但对于不需保密但有商业价值的国防专利,也加以推广运用。至 2000 年时,我国宣称国防专利局对民间向国家知识产权局申请的军用高级材料、军用元器件等 100 多件专利进行了保密扣压,防止了这些技术因向国内外公开而可能对国家安全造成的危

害；但也强调国防专利局也直接受理的专利案件约 1 500 多件，经审查得到专利权的约 1 100 件，其中有 51% 在特定范围得到了不同程度的推广应用，取得了明显的军事和经济效益。

所以，我国实行国防专利制度，以法律形式保护国防专利权人对其专利的占有权及使用权，以政府公权力介入民众的财产利益，具有推动国防现代化建设与发展国民经济的正当目的。同时我国也参考欧美先进国家的做法，对民众因专利被保密而产生的损失，由政府给予补偿。我国对国防专利的管理，兼顾国防机密的保护和国防技术转移需要；我国实行国防专利制度，在中央要求深化科技与经济体制改革的新形势下，日益显示生机和活力，并在"有利于维护国家安全和利益"、"有利于充分调动国防科技工业和军队有关部门科技人员从事发明创造的积极性"、"有利于国防专利技术成果向民用转移和军工产品与技术的出口"、"有利于促进国防科技成果推广应用"、"有利于提高军事武器装备质量和水平"、"有利于防止国防无形财产的流失"等六个方面作出了贡献。

从我国与美国的做法，到其他先进国家都有军事科技转移的政策，可以发现国际间对国防研发成果的保密管理趋势，不仅是单纯建立在国家或国防的保密法规基础上，还必须分析国防安全需求与国家经济利益的平衡，甚且要顾及原产权所有者的损失与政府补偿制度。因此，有效的国防科技保密制度不仅应植基在知识产权的形成与管理上，还应有利于成果转移于经济建设并产生效益。

第四章
美国国防科技保密的机制

美国为应对国防科技发展的商业化及全球化,将以往从二战到冷战期间所建立的"封闭式"(hermetic seal)保密做法调整为"免疫系统"(immune system)方式来保护国防科技机密。其所谓的免疫式的保密系统,是靠多重的法制系统与政策指示而紧密建构起来的;如同本书前一章所归纳的,可以区分为国家机密保护、国内科学技术(以下简称"国内科技")保密、国际科学技术(以下简称"国际科技")保密、商业秘密保护等四种法律系统,同时国防部依据这些法制,更以法规命令的方式制定执行面相关规范,并由跨部门整体运作。本章就美国这些法制规范分节作深入探讨。

第一节 国家机密保护机制

一、美国政府的国家机密保护机制

美国政府有系统建立国家机密法制,是在冷战时期从杜鲁门总统发布行政命令(Executive Order)要求对非军事信息作分类保密

第四章 美国国防科技保密的机制

起建立的,其后也均由总统发布行政命令进行增修,由行政机关遵守执行的。美国现行的国家安全信息的机密分类与保密制度,主要依据1995年4月17日由克林顿总统发布的12958号行政命令(Executive Order12958),将政府信息的机密分类分为"极机密"(top secret)、"机密"(secret)、"秘密"(confidential)三级。在美国遭遇9·11恐怖攻击后,布什总统于2003年3月15日发布13292号行政命令(Executive Order13292),作为12958号行政命令的增修规定,对于该第(e)项条文,在"与国家安全有关的科学、技术或经济事务"之后增列"包括防卫跨国性恐怖攻击"的字眼。

前文的总统行政命令,主要还是针对广泛性的政府信息保密需求,建立行政机关保密机制,各部门再据以制定各自的行政规则,形成国家机密保护体系。该命令中对于核定机密等级的权力、保密期间、机密标示、机密数据的使用、解密或降低机密等级的规定等,都有详细规定,因此而建立美国政府行政机关的国家机密维护体系。对于本书所关注的科学技术保密,也明订于机密信息类型之一,可见美国政府重视科学技术信息与国家安全有密切的关联性。至于特别针对科学技术信息的保密需求,则更早在Executive Order12958之前,里根政府时代即基于相同的维护国家安全的政策目的,于1985年9月21日颁布《第189号国家安全决定指令》(National Security Decision Directive 189,NSDD 189),规范各大学、实验室以联邦政府资金研发所产生的科学技术信息,基于国家安全的理由必须被管制,但属于基础研究的发现一般不会受到管制。NSDD 189主要是希望建立政府所资助的研发成果的管控机制,因此要求政府机关在出资赞助或委外作研究时,必须在签约前负责决定适当的保密做法和定期审查机密分类的做法。依据国家安全顾问Condoleezza Rice在2001年11月1日发布的文件,NSDD 189仍然有效,事实上也成为目前美国国内各大学、企业等从事科技研究的民间团体所遵守,并作为其单位内部进行科技信息管制或保密的依据。

二、敏感性但非属机密信息的保密做法

美国虽然通过总统的行政命令,建立了三级制的国家机密信息分类,但仍未能满足行政机关的保密需求,因此,在"极机密"、"机密"、"秘密"外,增设了敏感性但非属机密信息(sensitive but unclassified,SBU)的信息分类标示,其目的是使这些信息可以在行政机关内部流通使用但不被外界公众取得。行政机关所引用的 SBU 的保密区分,事实上没有在任何实体法规中被定义,但在 1984 年总统发布的《第 145 号国家安全决定指令》(National Security Decision Directive 145,NSDD – 145)中,曾指示对"敏感性但非属机密(SBU)的政府产生的信息,若外泄会影响国家安全利益,就必须对其运用产生的威胁和对国家安全的潜在危害的部分,加以保护"。该文件并未明确对 SBU 进行名词定义,但使用 SBU 的用语,主要是用来解释即使是非机密的信息,其集合起来仍可能显露高度机密或其他敏感的信息,会有害于国家安全利益。

至 1986 年 10 月 29 日,里根总统的国家安全顾问 John Poindexter 发布一份名为《联邦政府电子通讯及自动化信息系统中敏感性但非属机密信息的保护政策》(National Policy on Protection of Sensitive, but unclassified Information in Federal Government Telecommunications and Automated Information Systems,NTISSP No.2)的文件,扩大保护 SBU 的理论,指 NSDD – 145 中所称的国家安全目的包括"其他政府利益",同时对 SBU 提出定义为:"是指信息的披露、损失、误用、变更或破坏会对国家安全和其他政府利益有不利影响。"这份文件适用于所有联邦政府部门机关及其契约承包商间电子传递、贮存、处理、通讯的敏感性但非属机密信息。由于

适用范围太广招致批评，政府于 1987 年废止 NTISSP No.2 及其对 SBU 定义，另以《计算机安全法案》取代作为信息安全管理的法源依据。

此处提到行政机关使用 SBU 分类的做法，可说是美国整个国家机密保护机制中的灰色地带。由于科学技术研发的成果或相关信息，需具备该技术领域的专业知识基础才能了解，因此通常难以运用 Executive Order12958 定为保密的，往往会落入 SBU 的范围中，使得大学、企业或研究机构承包政府科研计划后，对于研发成果及数据是否可以发表或公开，造成很大困扰，成为美国国家安全维护对科技研发产生限制的重要来源。

三、白宫在 9·11 事件后的新政策

9·11 事件对美国国家安全产生巨大冲击，由于美国面临全球恐怖分子的威胁，关于个人权利及国家安全利益冲突的议题，便引起重大关注。美国政府的一些作为，例如，使用军事法庭审判嫌疑恐怖分子，司法部拘留超过 1 100 名非美国公民，为了扩张政府对人民监督权限通过《美国爱国者法案》（USA Patriot Act of 2001）及《国土安全法案》（Homeland Security Act of 2002），都引发了质疑或批评的声浪。其中《美国爱国者法案》赋予政府有更大的权限和弹性可以追捕恐怖分子，但也引起争议，例如，政府对海外美国公民的情报侦察、政府更易于取得图书馆等数据库的数据、对个人网站内容的监控等，都有可能成为司法部滥用使嫌疑者罪名成立的证据。而《国土安全法案》则包含一个所谓的"Davis – Moran proposal"（116 Stat. 2135.），要求民间交付政府的信息关系到国家基础设施安全的，不仅不能对外披露，政府也有权下令成为国家机密。

在这种潮流下，国家的法制与行政措施以国家安全名义，使政

府应保有更多秘密、限制民间产出的信息从公共领域发布等。而限制取得信息的方法,也被认为比保护信息内容本身更重要。2002年3月19日,白宫发布一份更著名的 Card 备忘录(由 Andrew H. Card, Assistant to the President and Chief of Staff, 署名发布),名为:《保护与国土安全有关的大规模破坏武器和其他敏感文件信息的行动》(Action to Safeguard Information Regarding Weapons of Mass Destruction and Other Sensitive Documents Related to Homeland Security),要求行政机关必须重新审视现有保护信息的方法,防止信息被误用而有害国家人民的安全,因此,需配合国家档案总署(National Archives and Records Administration)信息安全监督办公室(Information Security Oversight Office, ISOO)将必要的信息列为机密,包括以前认为非机密或已解密的信息,而且要将处理结果在90天内经国土安全办公室(Office of Homeland Security)向白宫报告。因此,政府单位对因特网上公开的文件进行检查。据统计仅从官方网站上就移除了6 000多件"敏感但非属机密"的文件。

而配合白宫这份文件,国家档案总署也发布一份备忘录,其中有一章节名称即为"敏感但非属机密信息",指示行政机关要保护"与美国国土安全有关的敏感性信息"(sensitive information related to America's homeland security, SHSI),并告知运用《信息自由法案》(FOIA)的豁免条款,尤其是第二款"机关内部人事规则和运作实务"及第四款"从他人处获得的商业秘密和商业、财务信息,基于个人权益需要保密"的规定,来排除信息披露的要求。

所以,可以看出美国政府在9·11事件之后,以国土安全的名义,运用 SBU 的做法,紧缩科技信息的管制。其所谓的"敏感但非属机密的国土安全信息"可以包括政府机关处理纪录、机关管理和监控的公共设施、某些内部数据库(报告、政府收集数据、地图等)、未定案的评估、某些内部的商议和民间公司提供给政府的信息等。科技研发活动和科技信息的流通,均因此受到影响。

第二节 国内科技保密法

国家机密保护法制,是以一般性的政府机密信息为管理保护对象,涵盖国防科技方面的研究成果与信息,但不是针对科技研发所设计的。美国另有一些法律,特别针对科技研究的成果与信息,防止其披露或外泄影响国家安全,而制定保密或管制的规范。

一、发明秘密法

(一)因战争需求产生的发明秘密法

美国在准备加入第一次世界大战时,为了保护公众安全和国防,防止研究发明的信息落入敌人手中,由国会于1917年10月6日通过《发明秘密法案》(Invention Secrecy Act),建立机密专利的制度。基于战时的需要,专利审查委员会有权对申请的专利下令保密,违反者有严厉的处罚,因此发明者无法公开其研究成果,更无从使用、实施或制造,当然损害专利权人应有的权益。国会也了解这种保密制度有两个问题,第一是发明人因此而降低将研究成果申请专利的意愿,不利于政府寻求潜在有用的研究发明;第二是法案内需要提供适当保护措施,才不会对专利权人的权利有所损害,所以该法案中提供一个补偿机制,以金钱补偿专利权人因为无法实施其专利所受的损失。该法案对于专利保密的期间限于战时,因为第一次世界大战在来年就结束了,因此大部分机密专利保密的命令仅持续1年,实际上对专利权人的影响极为有限。

在第一次世界大战结束后，美国专利保密的做法沉寂了20年的时间，直到美国准备再投入第二次世界大战时，于1940年7月1日对《发明秘密法案》进行了更新发布，恢复了1917年法案的大部分条款。当时美国尚未宣战，因此国会仅赋予了该法案2年的有效期限，但在2年后法案有效期限届满时，美国已经参战，因此1942年6月16日国会增修通过该法案在战争期间持续有效。由此可以看出1917年和1940年的法案所规定的专利保密制度，是为了战争目的而由国会授权行政部门行使。美国在第二次世界大战实施的专利保密制度，较第一次世界大战时更为严格，在1941年8月21日对1940年法案的增修条款中，不仅再次强调1917年所制定的专利保密措施，而且对于违反者处以更严厉的处罚，包括未经允许将机密专利公开或申请他国专利，发明人将丧失专利权并处罚最高1万美元罚金，若是故意行为经证明有罪，还必须处以拘禁的刑责。第二次世界大战期间，美国还建立起更周密的发布专利保密命令的程序，1940年8月专利审查委员会即要求陆军及海军设立"陆海军专利顾问委员会"（Army and Navy Patent Advisory Board, ANPAB），协助专利局决定哪些专利影响国家安全。在1948年该委员会更名为"军事服务专利顾问委员会"（Armed Services Patent Advisory Board, ASPAB），其后继续存在，并提供专利局作实质审查以决定是否发布专利保密命令的报告。

（二）战后和平时期演变为专利保密制度

在第二次世界大战结束后，美国专利审查委员会于1945年11月30日废止了大战期间所执行的6 575个专利保密命令，这些专利发明主要是因兼具军事及商业的价值，而被释出供专利权人做商业上的运用；但除此之外，在1945年底仍有799个专利基于军事上的理由继续处于保密状态，1949年9月23日前苏联宣布原子弹已经测试成功，紧接着1950年美国参与朝鲜战争，结果使机密专利

第四章　美国国防科技保密的机制

的数量在 1951 年又增长至 2 395 项之多。所以，国会在国防部一再游说之下，又在 1951 年通过新的《发明秘密法案》（Invention Secrecy Act of 1951），这次法案中有一个重要的改变，是明确在和平时期因被下令保密而不予核发专利的发明期限为 1 年，若仍有保密需要，应再由专利审查委员会审查后重新下令保密 1 年，这样确保机密专利能每年进行审查，以寻求在和平时期兼顾发明人和国家安全的利益。但该法案中也规定战时所发布的专利保密命令在战争期间及战争状态结束后 1 年内持续有效，以及在国家紧急状态所发布的专利保密命令在紧急状态时期及解除后 6 个月内持续有效。因为美国杜鲁门总统在 1950 年宣布国家进入紧急状态，直到 1979 年 3 月才正式解除紧急状态，因此，在 1979 年以前，实际上都没有执行过和平时期的专利逐年保密审查的做法。此外，1951 年的法案也扩大了发明人的权利，包括对保密命令不服的专利权人，可以向商务部长提出申诉；对申请国外专利的限制也降低，在申请美国专利 6 个月后，获有商务部许可即可申请国外专利；而对专利权人因为保密命令所受的损失，也允许其向行政部门提出补偿申请。

1951 年《发明秘密法案》所建立的这一套机制，就是利用专利制度来筛检政府机构和民间的研究成果。所以，针对专利申请案的技术内容，专利审查委员有责任在审查前预作考虑，公开后如果有害国家安全的，可以发布要求保密的命令。这套 1951 年《发明秘密法案》后来直接收录于美国专利法条文中（35USC§181-188），形成专利保密的规定，但其实被要求保密的，不仅包括专利本身申请范围，更涵盖完整的研发内容，且其他以前或以后提出申请的专利的主要部分落入此保密范围的，也受本命令的约束而必须保密。

所以，政府要能相当有效地掌握全国科技研发的成果信息，必须充分利用专利制度，使专利制度不仅用来保护发明人权益和促进科技进步,还可以具有管制信息及维护国家安全的功能。在美国提出专利申请必须在6个月之后,才能再申请国外专利,这6个月期间就是要供能源部(DOE)、国防部(DOD)及航天总署(NASA)等单位审查专利的内容,以确保专利权授与及技术内容公开不会影响国家安全。

在专利提出申请6个月内政府未下令保密,政府就无权再要求保密。但政府还可以通过强制、非专属的授权利用该专利技术,不需事先经专利权人同意,这称为"强制授权"(Compulsory License)。被强制授权的专利权人可以向相关政府机构寻求财务上的损害补偿,补偿金额的裁定通常是依据合理权利金标准加上因权利金延迟给付所生损害。

二、技术转移过程的科技保密

(一)拜杜法案

美国自1980年通过《拜杜法案》(Bayh – Dole Act, 1980),并陆续通过数项法案推动技术转移政策,使美国大学及研究机构可以直接将政府出资委托的研发成果归为己有,由学校或机构进行技术转移,从而带动产业科技创新的发展,并发挥创新的经济效益。《拜杜法案》等一系列推动技术转移法案的主旨就是积极将国有研发成果释放到民间,但美国政府也没有忘记保密的需要,在《拜杜法案》中就包含了保密条款,即35USC§205的规定:"对于联邦政府拥有或可能拥有一部分专利权、所有权或利益(含非专有的执照),联邦单位有权在相当时期内向社会大众保持缄默不宣告其发明成果,以便能够提出专利申请。特别的,联邦单位不得公开已向美国专利商标局提出专利申请,或已向任何外国专利主管机关提出申请的任何专利说明书及其相关申请数据。"结合前文已介绍的专利保密制度,加之美国政府释放到民间的研发成果已经过筛选,因此，美国政府在积极推动国有研发成果技术转移及商业化运用的同时，已利用相关的法令建立起保密机制，避免机密科技研发成果搭上技术转移的便车外流而影响国家安全。

（二）国家产业安全计划

美国由政府推动技术转移政策，就是要将国家的科技成果转移至民间，并在产业界加以应用。这种政策代表了一种政府科技信息释放的精神，但又不能与国家安全相悖，为了避免国家关键科技信息通过产业界外流，美国在立法或行政制度上，严格规范政府机构与产业界进行技转或合作的行为，对机密信息采取适当保护措施，并要求产业界对于政府释出的科技信息或成果必须加以管制或保密。

美国总统在1993年1月6日颁布第12829号行政命令，即《国家产业安全计划》（National Industrial Security Program，NISP），其目的就是要在政府机密信息向民间承包商、被授权者、被让与者释放时，对信息加以保护。因此，这项命令明确要求，基于国家利益，政府各部门在与民间单位签署执行可能涉及国家机密信息的契约、授权、让与等技术转移活动时，行政机关必须采取适当的保护措施。由此可见，NISP文件的精神是认为，国家安全利益是要发展产业以促进经济和技术进步，但必须兼顾保密需求。值得重视的是，以封闭式的信息保密管制，放弃与民间产业合作的机会，必然更易于维护国家安全，但美国政府并未对国家安全利益作狭义的定义，而能以更先进的思维推动技术转移，使国防与经济同步发展。这种技术转移过程中的保密需求与做法，不同于政府机关基于安全理由执行的内部保密控制和管理，由此可见，政府技术转移制度的成功与否，其衍生的保密制度占有关键性的地位。

（三）第2501条的规定

美国从《拜杜法案》起推动一系列的法案，建立政府技术转移制度，法案在各部门的业务工作中执行、推动，其中国防部的技术成果所占比例最大，也是最重要的单位。

在美国法典第十部中（US Code TITLE 10）即有关于军事武力的相关规定，第一百四十八章名为"国防科技和产业基础、国防转投资，和国防转化"（Chapter 148 – National Defense Technology and Industrial Base, Defense Reinvestment, and Defense Conversion），第2501条为"关于国家科技和产业基础的国家安全目的"，提到国家科技及产业政策支持国防科技武力发展，以达到国家安全目的。在第2537条中也规定"管制国防科技转移海外"，从这些规定都可以看到美国政府重视国防科技与产业发展的关联性，并同时要求确保国家安全。条文中虽然没有明确规定保密的做法，但国防部依据这些法律和前文NISP的要求，建立了国防科技保密制度和规则，由于国防部是美国政府执行技术转移最重要的部门，因此这些保密机制，不仅在国防部适用，有些还是跨部门运作或提供其他部门共同遵守的，这将留待本章第五节再加叙述。

三、其他有关法案

美国政府除了运用专利审查制度来筛检科技研发信息外，其他有关科技研发信息的披露会受到保密限制的，主要是落入本章第一节所述的"国家机密保护法制"的范围之中，包括前节所述的"技术转移过程的保密"，是针对程序上产生的需求及做法，保密的客体仍以"国家机密信息"为主。但其他一些与科技发展有关的个别法案中，仍会零星提到机密信息的产生和保密需求，对科技研发单位或人员也造成限制。

（一）原子能法案

美国在第二次世界大战期间秘密研发原子弹，参与的科学家很多都是非政府人员，由于执行了很严谨的保密措施，使得原子弹可以成功地秘密研发，取得最后战争胜利。战后在1946年国会通过了原子能法，设立原子能委员会（Atomic Energy Commission）并制定与原子能有关信息的安全政策。其实这正是国家机密保护法制中所谓"机密分类"（classified）的起源，而该法同时也创造了"限阅数据"（restricted data, RD）的分类，管制的范围包括民间的研究信息。起初这些信息只允许为国防目的获得，后来在1954年的修正法案（Atomic Energy Act of 1954）中，允许特定的非政府人员，如产业界专家、外国官员等，在取得安全认证后，基于原子能的和平商业化目的或国际合作计划而接触限阅数据。

RD的定义是，只要是有关于：（1）原子能武器的设计、制造或使用；（2）特殊核能原料的产制；（3）使用特殊核能原料产生能源，但不包括142［42 USC 2162］所排除的部分，所有信息均属于限阅。违反者可处以任何期限的徒刑，处以或同时处以100 000美元罚金。

（二）计算机安全法案

《计算机安全法案》（The Computer Security Act of 1987）在立法目的中即宣称："改进联邦政府计算机系统内'敏感性'信息是基于公共利益"，法案也授权国家标准局（National Bureau of Standards，现为National Institute of Standards and Technology, NIST）制定计算机标准，促进政府部门计算机系统的安全。所以，该法案是利用"敏感性信息"的名称来要求计算机通讯技术方面信息的保密，该法案对"敏感性"的定义为："任何信息的损失、误用、或未被授权取得或修改，会对国家安全或联邦政府计划的执行，以及对民众受隐私法所保障的个人隐私，有不利影响，但该信息又无法依政府行政命令或国会法案被列为影响国防或外交利益机密。"

所以，《计算机安全法案》的保密要求，还是要先服从国家机密保护法，但因计算机信息科技发展太快，运用政府既有的行政命令或法案来保密明显不足,需要扩大保密的范围。而为回避《信息自由法案》(FOIA)规定的政府信息披露义务,美国政府参考 FOIA 所列出的信息形态及定义,举出"对国家利益有不利影响"、"对联邦政府计划的执行有不利影响"和"隐私权"三个理由,来归类出所谓的"敏感性"信息,以符合 FOIA 的规定。NIST 在依据《计算机安全法案》执行政府信息系统安全工作的相关文件中,也都声明《计算机安全法案》并不与《信息自由法案》(FOIA)相抵触。在这种信息披露的限制下,也形成了一定程度的保密要求。

第三节

国际科技保密制度

一、美国主导国际间科技出口管制

本书第三章第二节所介绍的国际间科技出口管制条约,包括从二次世界大战以后的"多边出口管制协调委员会"(COCOM)转型到瓦圣那协议,及联合国禁止化学武器公约(CWC)等,都是由美国主导建立的。二次世界大战后,事实上美国继续发动了韩战、越战、冷战、波斯湾战争、反恐战争等,因此,通过国际间的科技出口管制协议,防止其国防科技对国家以外地区泄漏的保密机制,对维护美国国防科技优势、保障其国家安全具有重大意义。

美国的科技研究开发信息,除了在国内有法规要求保密或限制披露外,对于科技成果已经在其国内公开应用的,也采取措施对国外进行保密。因此,对于包含有高科技技术成分的产品出口,或技术本身要对国外进行转移,仍有可能在输出美国国土以外地区时受到管制。

二、美国政府的科技出口管制

美国政府的科技出口管制措施,除了依据前项的国际协约管制外,还制定了相关国内法来落实及执行管制工作。

(一) 出口管制规范

美国有关出口管制可能适用的法律、规章及管理监督的政府机构,可谓相当复杂。不仅在高科技产品实际离开美国本土时加以限制,而且对海外美国公司以及对在美国本土的非美国人也有很多管理措施,在美国本土的非美国人即使受雇于美国公司,也有很多管制措施限制其接触有关科技的研究开发。在法令方面,《出口管理法》(Export Administration Act)及商务部发布的《出口管理规则》(Export Administration Regulations,EAR)等,都有对出口产品、技术、出口地区及再出口的限制;出口管制主管机关主要是商务部,某些管制规定由国防部、财政部,乃至国务院或跨部委主管。另外,美国是前述瓦圣那协议发起国之一,故其出口也受该协议规范。

美国出口管理制度与瓦圣那协议等国际协约有相当密切的联结,但因为经济贸易活动的展开,执法过程中自然产生管制项目的公平性或合理性的争议,因此,美国国会及工商界均认为有必要对有关的管制加以简化或标准化。近几年来美国对出口管制的修正很多,最大的修正是已公开的技术产品不再受管制,有关技术、产品管制项目,也会做出定期检查,及时排除不须加以管制的项目。但美国在遭受9·11恐怖攻击之后,出口管制制度在执行面上立刻紧缩,趋于严厉,并被视为国家安全的重要一环进行评估。

整个国家科技信息管制,除了出口管制制度以外,还有以下的法案。

(二) 科学技术信息的出口管制规则

《出口管理法》(Export Administration Act) 和《武器出口管制法》(Arms Export Control Act) 都授权政府对科学技术数据出口进行管制,对项目的管制则依据《出口管理规则》(EAR) 或《国际间武器管制规则》(International Traffic in Arms Regulations, ITAR)。EAR 对"技术数据"(technical data) 的定义是:"可以被使用或运用在物品或材料的设计、生产、制造、利用、重建等任何形态的信息。这些数据可以是有形的,如模型、原型、蓝图、操作模型;或是无形的,如技术服务等。"ITAR 对"技术数据"(technical data) 的定义是:"与国防物品直接有关的设计、工程、发展、生产、处理程序、制造、使用、操作、拆检、修理、维修、改良或重建的信息。包括下列例示形式的信息:蓝图、草图、照片、计划、指令、计算机软件和文件等。也包括可以增进美国军火清单所列项目的技艺状态的信息,但不包括一般性科学、数学或工程原理的信息。"所以,ITAR 是管制美国军火清单(22 CFR 121)上所列项目及其相关技术,EAR 是管制商务部管制清单上(15 CFR Part 774)的军民两用物品及其相关技术。被管制物品要出口都必须先申请并取得核准。主管 EAR 并核发出口许可的是商务部,主管 ITAR 及美国军火清单并核发出口许可的是国务院(Department of State),不论民间或政府资助所产生的科学技术数据均属于被管制范围,但不包括基础研究信息。

ITAR 将技术资料的披露或转移给外国人均视为技术出口,不论是在美国境内或国外。研究人员都知道在美国进行科技研发要与外国人员举行会议或研讨时,都必须先向国务院申请,ITAR 对纯粹属于学术性、公开领域的科学技术信息交流是排除管制的。然而这种界限并不明确,许多学术研究机构执行的研究计划若用到太空、国防等科技,还是必须注意管制问题。

自1999年起,有关卫星和太空载具仪器等技术数据和相关讨论,也都被列到国务院的ITAR的管辖之下。部分学者抱怨他们参加会议、校园内研究和国际合作的机会大为减少,而大学内外国籍研究员和学生要取得这类相关信息也受到限制,最终大学要求主管机关阐明法律的规定和依据。因此,国务院在2002年3月颁布的新规定中,对于某些在公开领域中特定的太空基础研究信息,输出给北约成员国、欧盟或欧洲太空总署、非北约成员国等主要友邦(如日本、以色列)的大学或研究中心,可以免除ITAR的管制。同时允许非机密的科学研究产品或实验卫星等组装技术数据出口,但对于卫星或太空载具的整合发射系统或导弹技术管制条约(Missile Technology Control Regime,MTCR)管制的项目仍不许出口。对于已豁免管制的技术数据和硬件若要出口到非豁免管制的国家,仍需申请许可。此外,获得输出许可的国外合作研究单位,必须保证其单位内未经许可的研究人员不能取得限制性的信息。

第四节

商业秘密法

知识产权法律体系通常要求科学技术成果的发明人或拥有人将技术内容公开,由政府赋予发明人或拥有人财产权利,并运用政府权力加以保护,但"商业秘密"法则是例外。为了保护更大的经济利益,"商业秘密"法允许科技研发信息保持秘密。业界对于研发成果选择使用专利或商业秘密来保护,取决于许多因素,包括产品具有竞争优势的生命周期、使用商业秘密保护的成本与风险、证明专利侵权的困难性、竞争者模仿的困难程度等。例如，如果竞争者只要购买产品再通过逆向工程就可以轻易仿制的技术，那么申请专利保护较有利；若是技术内容披露后要证明专利侵权较困难（如制造方法专利），则应考虑以商业秘密保护。这种业界所普遍熟悉且愿意自发性采取的保密行为，显然是政府针对"科技保密"的应对方法，本节即就美国的商业秘密法，及利用保护"商业秘密"的方法所制定的《经济间谍法案》，作简要介绍。

一、美国商业秘密法

商业秘密在对象定义及权利范围界定的困难非常突出。但国家既然要创设出商业秘密这样一个权利，来保护科学技术研发成果，就必须对保护对象加以严格定义或指出构成要素。美国在 1939 年《侵权行为法汇编》（Restatement of Torts, §757）即规定："商业秘密包含可以运用在商业上的任何程序、形态、装置或处理过的信息，其拥有者在竞争对手未知悉或未运用之前，可以保持竞争优势。所以，它可以是化合物的反应方程式、制造程序、材料处理保存方法、机器或装置的形态、顾客名单等。它不同于其他商业上的所谓的秘密信息，因为这些信息仅是针对商业运作上的单一或短暂的事件，例如，秘密采购标案的契约中提到的数量、某些雇员的薪资、投资计划中的秘密资料、宣布新政策的日期、预计实施新商业模式的时间等。因此，商业秘密是商业运作上可以连续使用的程序或装置，一般而言，它是与商品的生产有关的，例如，某项货品生产的机器或方程式。商业秘密也可能和商品的销售或其他商业运作有关，如决定折扣的计算方法、价格回馈方式、特殊客户名单、订位方法或其他管理方法等。"

不过《侵权行为法汇编》是由早期判例法归纳而来，规范内容过于抽象，且后来美国各州依据联邦法院判例，纷纷立法对商业秘密加以保护,因此,美国法律学会于1978年修编时删除了上述商业秘密的规定。但是各州因产业发展情况不一,造成各行其政的情况,因此,由"统一州法全国委员会"(National Conference of Commissioners on Uniform State Laws)于1979年拟订通过《统一商业秘密法》,建议各州采用。原则上该法仅对侵害商业秘密的民事责任加以规定,至于刑事责任,则仍建议各州自行规范。《统一商业秘密法》中则将商业秘密定义为:"包含方程式、形态、编辑物、计算机程序、装置、方法、技术或程序等任何信息,这些信息在不被他人广泛知悉、不被他人轻易获得的情况下,具有事实上或潜在的独立经济价值;而且这些信息必须尽合理的努力保持其秘密性。"此定义基本上沿袭《侵权行为法汇编》的定义,但有几点不同:(1)《统一商业秘密法》明文规定商业秘密是任何"信息",但《侵权行为法汇编》则未明确写入条文;(2)《统一商业秘密法》所例示的商业秘密形态比《侵权行为法汇编》要多;(3)《侵权行为法汇编》强调商业上的连续使用性,但《统一商业秘密法》并无此条件;(4)《侵权行为法汇编》要求商业秘密是具有"竞争优势",但《统一商业秘密法》则强调"事实上或潜在的独立经济价值"。

当然,美国是一个习惯法国家,其联邦及州的立法和判决均可以对商业秘密的定义加以阐释。例如,FOIA中对于商业上需要保密的信息有免除披露的规定,在大多数案例中,法院解释这类信息都会运用《侵权行为法汇编》和《统一商业秘密法》有关商业秘密的定义。但近来有两个判决,巡回法院未引用《侵权行为法汇编》和《统一商业秘密法》而采用更狭隘的定义。有些州则采用刑法上偷窃商业秘密罪的定义。

不论是《侵权行为法汇编》和《统一商业秘密法》,"秘密性"(secrecy)都是判别是否为商业秘密的最重要因素。法院对商业秘密的认定,对"秘密性"的要求也甚于其他如"竞争优势"、"商业上连续使用"等条件。《侵权行为法汇编》和《统一商业秘密法》都没有对"秘密性"有明确的定义,但法院在实务处理上已有相当的经验,一般而言,判断是否符合秘密性必须考虑以下因素:(1)在企业以外,人们一般了解的程度;(2)商业秘密拥有者维持信息的秘密性所使用的保密措施的级别;(3)他人运用不当方法取得或复制信息的难易程度。所以,要符合"秘密性",信息拥有者对保密所作的努力,包括保密的方法、工具等,都占有很重要而关键的地位。

由于运用专利权、著作权保护需要将研发成果信息公开,使用商业秘密已成为科技产业界保护研发成果的另一项重要选择,商业秘密法也成为知识产权法制中重要的一环。但是基于其私隐性,政府无法事前进行"商业秘密"的审查而给予所有者一定范围的权利,因此,商业秘密法通常属于私法性质,并没有以行政机关的公权力介入审查、争端解决、援助等程序,而纯由民法侵权行为处理的居多,这对本书所要论述的"政府研发成果"保密,在性质的适用上有很大不同。但因商业秘密的做法对于科技研发信息及成果的保密,有非常重要的作用,因此,政府对国有科技研发成果的保密,也应该有很大的参考价值。以下介绍的美国《经济间谍法案》,就是运用商业秘密的观念,将政府公权力介入企业的知识产权保护,但其背后的立法目的,则与维护国家安全和经济利益有关。

二、美国经济间谍法案

美国国会在 1996 年 10 月通过了《经济间谍法案》(The Economic Espionage Act,简称 EEA),法案的主要目的是以政府的公权力来保障私人企业的知识产权。《经济间谍法案》可以分为两大部分:第一部分是针对外国政府或其代理人的商业间谍行为;第二部分则是针对一般国内的商业间谍行为。

该法以保护企业的商业秘密为法制范畴，将原本由各州以习惯法（Common Law）中的不正当竞争禁止原则等各自处理的商业秘密案件，通过联邦的立法及附加刑罚的规定，快速且有效地保护其在私法上的商业秘密。

《经济间谍法案》对于"商业秘密"作出了如下的定义：它属于任何形式与种类的金融、商业、科学、技术、经济、或工程方面的信息；其中包括机制形态、计划书、出版物、程序设计、配方、设计图、模型、制造方法与技术、处理程序与制造过程、计算机程序、密码等。不论该信息是有形或无形、或其储存及收集的方式（电子、图案、照片或文字）均可被视作为商业秘密。可知该定义几乎已经包括了一切有形与无形的知识产权。

美国《经济间谍法案》是联邦刑事法，一旦被告被判决确定就将会面临着被监禁及罚款的可能。一方面，《经济间谍法案》与美国一般的刑事法相比，其管辖权范围比较广，同时对犯罪的处罚也比较严厉；这主要是因为美国国会希望用《经济间谍法案》来打击外国政府所支持的商业间谍活动以保障美国的国家安全。另一方面，由于《经济间谍法案》的另一个目的是希望以政府的权力来保护私人企业的商业机密，因而造成《经济间谍法案》的某些条款在保障私人的经济利益前提下与一般的刑事法精神大异其趣。

所以，美国《经济间谍法案》是采用知识产权的法律原则，但运用政府权力，附加刑法的功能，介入民间科技研究开发的保密事务。在一般知识产权如专利、商标与著作权的侵害案件中，都是由权利人自行诉讼，获取证据较为困难，但在《经济间谍法案》中，当企业主发现他人侵害其商业秘密，可以向联邦调查局反映，由其动用国家资源进行追缉。但探讨《经济间谍法案》背后的立法目的，绝非单纯为保障民间企业的商业秘密而已，能够使美国投入联邦政府资源，并且动用刑法制度，主要还是针对有外国政府在背后支持的经济间谍活动。所以,从美国司法部在立法时也特别强调将"国家安全"与"经济安全"画上等号的倾向看,《经济间谍法案》确实有保障美国的科技研究与发展,进而确保美国国家安全的目的。这种立法目的与做法,对本书所探讨的政府介入科技研究开发保密的课题,实具有一定的启示。

第五节　国防科技保密规范

以上在第一至四节所介绍的四种法律系统,基本上都与国家安全目的及其衍生的科学技术信息保密需求有关,因此,美国国防部执行国防科技方面的保密工作,均将上述四类法制作为法律授权依据,尤其在前三类法制之中,包括立法及执行,国防部均扮演主要及关键的角色。美国国防部在执行面上,也制定了许多规范。这些规范正是特别针对国防科技保密需求所制定的,因此,值得本书深入了解。

美国国防部为业务执行的需要,发布大量的"指令"(Directive)或"指示"(Instruction)的文件,作为指挥所属各单位运作的依据。"指令"属政策上的指导文件,包括依法律、总统与部长的要求,建立政策、计划和组织,并对任务进行定义、制定权限和职责等;"指示"则是补充这些政策的做法、行动、操作程序和相关职责等。这些文件中,有些就是特别针对国防科技保密需求制定的。

一、国防部信息安全计划

美国国防部于1996年12月13日发布的第5200.1号指令

第四章 美国国防科技保密的机制

(DOD Directive 5200.1)，名称为《国防部信息安全计划》(DOD Information Security Program)，是依据 Executive Order 12958 所要求的国家安全机密信息政策，制定适用于国防部内各单位的补充性规定。所以，这份文件是美国国家机密保护法制的一环，对机密信息的定义、范围、核定权责等规定，均与 Executive Order 12958 一致，例如，在该指令第 2-301 条中关于机密信息的类型，即直接引用 Executive Order 12958，第（e）项也是"与国家安全有关的科学、技术或经济事务"。

这份指令文件对于国防部的保密工作程序，有详尽的规定。全文共分十章，第一章叙述政策及计划管理基本要求；第二、三章是原始（Original Classification）及衍生（Derivative Classification）的机密等级的核定程序及做法；第四章是解密与降低机密等级的规定；第五章是机密标示的规定；第六章是机密信息保密的做法；第七章是针对机密信息交付或传递的规定；第八章规范特殊接触机密信息的计划；第九章是安全教育与训练；第十章则规范机密信息已实际泄漏或潜在可能泄漏的处理方式。

1997 年 1 月国防部由副部长签署发布一份《信息安全计划》(Information Security Program) 的指导文件（DOD 5200.1-R），使用了"仅为官方使用"(For Official Use Only, FOUO) 的分类，以运用在非属机密但需要保护的信息。该文件指 FOUO 包含：FOIA 之下可以免除向大众的信息披露责任的信息、国务院设计仅限官方使用的敏感但非属机密信息（SBU）、必须有正当的政府目的所持有的信息。并且要求所属单位对 FOUO 的使用限于："……在国防部单位之间，和国防部官员与其承包商、顾问、被授权者等需要执行国防事务人员之间。FOUO 信息可以为了执行正确的政府功能而释放给其他的行政和司法体系部门。提供 FOUO 给国会议员依据 DOD 5400.4 号指令，提供 FOUO 给会审总局依据 DOD 7650.1 号指令。"

美国陆军第 380-19 号规则第 1-5 节也指出:"SBU 的例子有:(a)涉及情报活动(b)涉及国家安全的密码活动的信息(c)涉及武力的指挥和管制的信息(d)信息中包含武器系统或武器中具有整体系统性的部分(e)信息中包含对直接完成军事或情报任务具有关键性的系统(f)涉及研究、发展和工程数据的处理程序的信息。"其核定为 SBU 的权限,最极致的情况可以授权到数据的拥有者或创造者自行决定。

二、国家产业安全计划作业手册

本章第二节中已提到 1993 年 1 月 6 日克林顿总统发布第 12829 号行政命令,实施《国家产业安全计划》(NISP),由"国家安全委员会"(National Security Council)负责制定 NISP 的整体政策和指示,国防部长负责执行,"信息安全监督局"(Information Security Oversight Office, ISOO)局长负责制定结合各部门共同执行的相关指令,以落实及监督 NISP。因此,国防部依据该命令的要求及授权,制定《国家产业安全计划作业手册》(National Industrial Security Program, Operational Manual, NISPOM)以说明政府机构向承包商披露政府机密信息(包括特殊分类的保密信息,如 Restricted Data、Formerly Restricted Data、情报来源和方法的信息、Sensitive Compartmented Information、Special Access Program 信息等),应防止非法披露及管制合法披露所必需的各项要求、限制披露的其他防护措施。这些程序适用于被授权人(licensees)、被让与人(grantees)和依法合格持有者。

NISP 既是为了执行国防科技(或是与国家安全有关科技)转移至民间产业化的政策,又是为防止机密科技成果外流,因此,依据第 12958 号总统行政命令施行的国家机密保护机制和相关法规建立。NISPOM 虽由国防部制定,但由国防部、能源部、核能规则委员会和中央情报局共同发布,这四个部门在手册中合称"审认安全机构"(Cognizant Security Agency, CSA),即除了联邦政府各部门依据第 12958 号总统行政命令必须对其内部信息进行认定和控管外,上述四个 CSA 有权另行认定政府与产业合作事项中何为机密,并执行有关于这些机密性活动或契约的安全行政工作,包括对执行计划的人员与设备进行查核及许可。

所以,NISPOM 适用于承接政府机构的契约或计划的民间承包商,在契约执行、授权、让与过程的各阶段,包括招标、协商、决标、执行时,对政府披露的机密信息进行保护。该手册同时适用于契约、授权、让与及提供外国政府信息予承包商时,所披露的虽非属机密信息,但基于国家安全利益仍有保护需求的信息的保密。所以,该手册可说是参照联邦法规、总统行政命令、政府指示、国际条约和特定政府机构间协议,针对国防科技产业化发展的综合性的补充规定,所有获得批准承接政府合约的承包商,都必须执行手册内的保密规定,其位于美国管辖领土内的场所设施都必须按规定接受检查。

三、《国防部对研究及技术保护的规定程序》草案

2001 年的 9·11 事件后,美国政府加强对科学技术信息的管制,国防科技更是重中之重。本章第一节已提到,美国联邦政府在 9·11 事件之后规定,接触到机密资料的政府机构现职及已离职雇员,或承接政府计划的人员,当要以私人名义发表科学技术信息时,实施"公开前审查"的机制。因此,国防部在其资助或委托外部研究的契约上,虽都已有"公开前审查"的条款,规定国防部要对研究信息公开发表前先进行审查;但配合政府加强科技信息管制的政策,国防部也在 2002 年 2 月发表了《国防部对研究及技术保护的规定程序》(Mandatory Procedures for Research and Technology Protection

Within the DOD)草案,要求研究人员对军方资助的研究成果,即使不属于机密资料,也必须经过国防部审查同意,才能公开讨论或发表。这样的规定已逾越了既有制度的规范,对科技信息交流产生极大冲击,因此引起学术界反对,国防部只得暂时撤回草案,但仍计划在定出更明确标准后提出新规定版本。

总之,除了前文提到的国防部制定的科技保密重点文件外,国防部及其所属单位还制定了许多相关的细节规定,并且随时依据国家安全防卫上的需求,不断地检讨保密制度及措施,才建构起完整的国防科技保密制度。

第六节

美国国防科技保密机制简评

由以上所介绍的法令制度可以了解,在美国从事科技研发,并非一般人所想像的可以自由而开放地进行信息交流,反而在不同的法律系统中受到各种的限制。美国政府整体的科技信息保密法令,都是以国家安全为核心,围绕国防科技发展所建立起来的,因此,国防部扮演核心和主导的角色,并对相关法令再出台补充规定,因此通常不仅是针对国防部内部而已。能源部、航天总署等部门,都属于国防科技发展的单位,都必须遵守国防科技保密规定。

重要的是,依这些法规授权的组织单位,例如,前文 NISPOM 中对于其所指定的国防部、能源部、中情局、核能规则委员会等四个 CSA,也授权其相关安全行政工作可以由 CSA 再进一步指定一个或数个"审认安全办公室"(Cognizant Security Offices,简称 CSO)负责,产业界执行政府合约或计划,就必须找到相对应的 CSO 接

第四章 美国国防科技保密的机制

受安全查核和控管事宜。

美国国防科技保密机制需要如此繁复的法令与组织系统来运作,主要是为了执行政府的技术转移政策。国防科技的研究开发多由政府出资进行,为了保密,大可在政府内部设置研发机构进行,这也是一般国家于刚开始发展国防科技时会采取的做法。但美国则能从经济效益及科技进步的角度考虑,将国防科技研发委托民间执行,并推动民间产业将这些研发成果商业化,这也使机密信息外流的机会和渠道大幅增加。

因此,探讨美国国防科技法令制度,不应仅是从被动的保密角度看待,而应从整体技术转移制度来观察。在1993年的美国《国防授权法案》(National Defense Authorization Act for Fiscal Year 1993)中,明文要求国防部长须设立"技术转移办公室"(Office of Technology Transition),该法案条文收录于 10 USC sec.2515 中,对于"技术转移办公室"明订五项任务,前二项即为:(1)监控所有与军事部门和国防机构有关的研发活动实施;(2)确认所有研发活动所使用的技术或造成的技术进步是否具有潜在非国防的商业化应用的可能。因此,国防部的各技术转移单位,实际上均根据科技发展和武器装备更新代换的情况,对军用技术进行技术转移研究,先行区分保密与否,对于不须保密科技成果则分期分批宣布解密,转为民用。所以,真正保密效果需重视技术转移源头的筛选制度,这有赖于整体科技研发与技术转移执行单位的配合,以使技术转移与保密协调,才能有效达到保密目的。

第五章

国防科技保密机制建设争议与问题

第一节 美国政府实施科技保密的法制争议

从前一章介绍的美国法制系统看,美国政府以国家机密保护、国内科技保密、国际科技保密和商业秘密保护(《经济间谍法案》)四大类法律系统为基础建立规范,或形成法律授权,再进一步制定补充性或执行层面的规则,建构完整而缜密的国防科技保密机制。这四类法律制度虽基于国家安全考虑,在立法目的上具有正当性,但因可能造成对科技发展的阻碍,以及对人民权利的限制,因此仍有许多争议。本节就美国各类法制产生的争议加以整理探讨。

一、国家机密保护法制的争议

(一)对政府机密核定的争议

根据美国宪法第一增修条文所反映的价值观,美国形成保障言

第五章 国防科技保密机制建设争议与问题

论自由及要求政府信息公开的社会风气,常见许多应属政府机密的信息被媒体披露或公开流传都没有受到司法制裁,而因特网等科技发展也使许多官方资料更易于被民众取得。

但另一方面,美国也是最有机密性的国家。政府每年所投入的巨额军事预算和庞大的情报机构开支,所产生的国家机密远超过任何一个国家。以1999年为例,就产生了8 038 592个新的机密,每年还以约10%的增长率增加,被授权可以核定国家机密的官员总数达3 846人。

因此,美国国家机密制度的首要争议,就是政府对机密的核定是否过滥。美国有学者指出,所谓"国家机密"包含可能影响国家安全的各种信息形态,但可以大致区分成三类:

1. 名副其实的国家安全机密(Genuine national security secrecy):是指那些信息内容泄漏后确实会对国家安全产生损害的信息。虽然对于何谓"国家安全"、何谓"损害"?很难明确定义,但一般可以认同的如先进军事技术的设计细节、情报功能机构运作的信息等,都属于此类机密。这类信息绝对有高度敏感性,是国家保密系统中优先要保护的对象。

2. 政治上的秘密(Political secrecy):此类秘密的形成是基于政治上的利益,并没有影响国家安全的顾虑,其目的是要保护官员或争议性高的计划,以免受到公众的责难和批评等困扰。这类的秘密在数量上应该最少,但却对国家政治的健全最有伤害。例如,早期核能研究造成民众受到辐射污染的资料被保密,事实上是为了逃避民众争议和法律责任。

3. 官僚式的秘密(Bureaucratic secrecy):是指因政府机构的官僚习性而不自觉所产生的秘密,既不影响国家安全,也没有政治上的利益可言。这种杂乱无章的官僚式秘密在现行国家保密系统上随处可见,许多机密档案内的数据存放了二三十年都未被审视过,还一直被视为是国家机密。

显然，美国政府对于国家机密的核定仍广受质疑，许多具有特殊政治性目的的秘密，或官僚系统散漫而未能解密的过时秘密，充斥于国家机密系统，使国家机密的公信力与运作受到伤害。

（二）对敏感性信息管制的争议

对于未列入成为国家机密信息，但又可能与国家安全有关的，美国政府仍可能使用"敏感但非属机密"（SBU）的标示，前文已提到行政机关使用 SBU 分类的做法，可说是美国整个国家机密保护机制中的灰色地带，更对大学、企业或研究机构承包政府科研计划后研发成果及数据发表或公开，形成很大困扰。而 9·11 事件后白宫所发布的 Card 备忘录和国会通过的《美国爱国者法案》（USA Patriot Act of 2001）及《国土安全法案》（Homeland Security Act of 2002）等，要求行政机关要保护"与美国国土安全有关的敏感性信息"（sensitive information related to America's homeland security, SHSI），更趋向于紧缩政府对信息的管制。

对于这类具有敏感性但未被列入国家机密的信息，因为行政机关对 SBU 的政策目的与定义用法均不一致，使信息保护与否取决于行政机关的决定，因此，基于国家安全目的和基于促进公众监督与科技发展的不同立场，当然引发一些争议。

1. SBU 政策的争议。美国于 1977 年由官方文件提出 SBU 的概念，其后则在许多行政命令或法案分别提到，但政府在国家机密保护的体制外，是否有必要再利用 SBU 来管制保密，以及 SBU 是否范围过当，都是这项政策的争议所在。有人认为行政机关应广泛解释 SBU，以保护更多的信息。例如，1994 年 2 月 28 日一份由"联合安全委员会"（Joint Security Commission）提供给中央情报局（CIA）主管和国防部长，名为《重新定义安全》（Redefining Security）的报告，宣称依据"美国科学家协会"（Federation of

第五章　国防科技保密机制建设争议与问题

American Scientists, FAS）在冷战后第一次全面调查政府安全政策和运作，估计政府所持有的信息中有多达 75% 都是属于敏感性但非属机密的。报告中强烈建议应该花费更大心血在国防、情报和其他政府部门保护这类信息并标示为 SBU。但另一方面，1997 年由 Moynihan commission 提出一份报告则指出，行政机关广泛运用多种不同型式的方法保护非机密信息，结果每个公务员几乎都可以自行决定哪些信息必须被管制，缺乏对这些分类和政府管控做法的监督机制，所以，其结论认为有过多的信息被保护。

2. SBU 的定义不明确。在 9·11 事件之前，SBU 的分类仅是政府对未符合 EO12958，但又希望限制公开的信息的标示。但新颁布的 EO13292 则将 SBU 扩大到科技信息范畴，以防范恐怖攻击。

但 SBU 并没有在实体法中定义，在某些法案中（如 Computer Security Act）已有"敏感性"（sensitive）的用语和管制作为，以排除《信息自由法案》（FOIA）和《隐私法》（Privacy Act）的适用，但这些法律对于哪些信息需要保护并没有明确定义，而是交由政府机关自行解释和风险评估。因此，政府机关在其补充规定和行政规则上所提到的 SBU 也就有许多不同的含义，有些机关也使用其他名词，如"仅官方使用"（for official use only）、"限制使用"（limited use）、"敏感性"（sensitive）等，或参考《隐私法》（Privacy Act of 1974, 5USC 552a）、《信息自由法案》（FOIA of 1966）、《计算机安全法案》（Computer Security Act of 1987, relevant portions codified at 15 USC 278 g-3）的文字来自行定义 SBU。SBU 因此缺乏明确的定义广受批评，包括会审总局（General Accounting Office，GAO）官员在国会中作证时也指出 SBU 需要明确的定义。

在 1997 年"保护及减少政府机密委员会"的一份报告指出，至少有 52 种标示被用在非属机密的文件上，其中较常用的就是 SBU、"限官方使用"（Limited Official Use）、"仅官方使用"（Official

Use Only）等。在9·11恐怖攻击之后，布什政府又要求行政机关在 FOIA 之下加强对有关国土安全和防范恐怖攻击的保密措施，使得行政部门对敏感性信息的运作更为复杂。

使用 SBU 分类应有两个原因：一方面是要尽量减少机密的数量；另一方面是向特定个人或团体传递一些具有敏感性但又必须让对方知道的信息。但是，政府机关为了本身的特定目的，用了许多不同方式来定义 SBU，始终缺乏政府整体统一性的规定，使得审定及管制的标准不一，招致极大争议。

3. SBU 与政府信息公开的冲突。行政机关使用 SBU 未在实体法上有明确规范，这种限制政府信息披露及流通的做法，和美国强调政府信息公开的精神有明显冲突。

美国《信息自由法案》（FOIA）的立法目的，就是要确保民众可以取得政府机关的相关信息，但有9种形态的信息是可以排除的：

（1）影响国防和外交利益的机密信息；

（2）机关内部人事规则和运作实务；

（3）法规规定不需披露的信息；

（4）从他人处获得的商业秘密和商业、财务信息，基于个人权益需要保密的；

（5）政府跨部门间或机关内部讨论尚未形成政策的文件；

（6）私人的、医疗的和类似档案，其披露明显侵犯个人隐私的；

（7）法律施行所指定形态的记录或信息；

（8）财务机构的规则或监督报告；

（9）关于矿井的地质或地理的信息。

所以，美国的法案或行政机关规定中，提到有关 SBU 的定义或使用时，凡较严谨的都会运用 FOIA 的豁免规定。如《计算机安全法案》就是参考 FOIA 所列出的形态,在下定义时,举出"对国家利益有不利影响"、"对联邦政府计划的执行有不利影响"和"隐私权"三个理由,来归类出所谓的"敏感性"信息,以符合《信息自由法案》(FOIA)的规定。国家标准技术院(NIST)在依据《计算机安全法案》执行政府信息系统安全工作的相关文件中,也都声明《计算机安全法案》与《信息自由法案》(FOIA)并不抵触。

虽然大多数的联邦政府机关都必须依据《计算机安全法案》的"敏感性"定义和《信息自由法案》(FOIA)所排除的信息类别,来执行或标示 SBU,但这些机关是否真的有权限自行认定排除 FOIA 的适用范围,仍遭受质疑。尤其在 9·11 事件后白宫所发布的卡德备忘录(CardMemo,2002 年 3 月),为了防范恐怖分子的攻击,指示行政机关扩张 FOIA 免除披露的信息形态和范围,更引起学者的批评和警告。

例如,有学者就质疑该备忘录对信息产生很多新的限制,根本不符合现行的 FOIA 法律架构,或是规范政府安全的机密与解密的 EO12958 的制度。2002 年 3 月 9 日《经济学家》的报道也提出警告,认为 SBU 是一种最危险层次的秘密,因为它以前从未被定义,也没有申诉或援助的渠道。另外,也有文章批评政府实施 SBU 缺乏行政援助机制,联邦政府要将此政策推动成功,必须尽快建立程序,让民众有不服政府信息管制决定的时候,有能力提出异议或寻求援助。因此,基于公众利益及信息公开的原则,包括 SBU 如何判别的要素、申诉的程序、扩大管制影响的评估、对基础研究的信息管制如何授权判定等许多议题,均引起国会和各界的重视。

(三)改革的呼吁

针对国家机密和 SBU 的制度运作可能对人民权益造成伤害,国会和民众提出了以下几项要求改革的方向和做法。

1. 扩大解密的权限。现行的国家机密制度是最初核定机密等级的官员才有解密的权限,这种做法是造成官僚式秘密和政治上秘密泛滥的原因,因此,除了当初核定机密的官员外,扩大其他官员可以根据实际情况获得解密的权限,才是减少官僚式秘密和政治上秘密的方法。所以,有学者主张设置独立于原来核定机关的外部的组织来审议,引进"外部成员",包括其他政府部门或民间公正客观人士等,参与机密审议委员会的评估,这样可以避免既有利益者的官僚习性,建立解密程序的公正性。这种做法已经在1996年政府设立的"跨部门安全机密等级审议会"(Interagency Security Classification Appeals Panel)中得到小规模的试用,在审议过的150余件案例中,有超过半数推翻原始核定机密机关的意见而予以完全解密。因此,在现行的保密制度上,应该要引进这种内部自我检查的机制,减少不必要的机密。另有学者则建议在属于行政体系的信息安全监督办公室(ISOO)接受申诉案件进行审议,解决争端,ISOO通过审议案件,可以了解不同机关间的立场和做法,得出较平衡的保密政策。

2. 加强司法审查。不仅在行政部门要扩张解密权限,司法部门也应有加强解密的功能,例如,以往法院在听审有关《信息自由法案》(FOIA)案件时,只要涉及国家安全机密的,大部分法官多未探究信息本身机密的必要性,而尊重或听从行政部门的意见。事实上法院更应该运用实体法上的"平衡原则"(balancing test),考虑公众利益和国家安全的需要作出保密与否的裁定,这不仅是法院维护本身司法审查的功能,也是建立国家机密制度的外部检查机制。

3. SBU 制度的检讨。SBU 所产生的定义问题、判别的要素、申诉的程序,以及以反恐和国土安全名义扩大管制的影响评估等,其争议已毋庸赘述,学者或民众期望政府能建立一致性的定义和明确规定,并不断制定补充配套措施,包括行政援助程序。

二、国内科技保密法制的争议

(一) 专利保密命令的争议

美国在专利法制度中实施保密命令的制度,在2002预算年度中,统计有效的机密专利数量达4 792件,其中大多数是由政府单位自行提出及拥有的专利,只有37件是对民间提出的专利下令保密。这些由民间自行研发申请专利而被下令保密的件数比例并不高,但却是主要争议的所在,其争议点如下:

1. 发布保密命令的决定是否已考虑发明人立场。保密命令审查与处分的合理性,主要是行政机关审查时是否有滥用行政权,扩大解释国家安全利益的范围,而影响发明人应有权益的情况。美国专利法规定,当政府对发明具有财产权时,行政机关的审查标准为"可能有害于国家安全",此处的"可能"代表一个最低的标准,行政机关有相当大的裁决权认定与国家安全有关。但是,当政府对该发明不具有财产权时,若仍对发明人发布保密命令,此时按法规应采用较严格的审查标准,即采用"将有害于国家安全"的标准。美国在第二次世界大战结束以后的和平时期,照理说战争威胁日益降低,但其对私人发明发布保密命令的数量却仍稳定增加,因此引起较大争议,包括有主张该规定在程序上应更加严谨、国会应要求行政机关建立更严谨且符合时宜的审查标准,以保障发明人。

2. 保密命令的法律效力是否公平合理。保密命令对发明人产生法律上强制效果,包括发明内容不得公开和违反时的处罚。

(1) 保密命令的有效期限。和平时期发布的保密命令有效期限为1年,届满若有需要保密再重新发布,"1年"的期限是否合理?依据法规的精神,既然是有害国家安全才被要求保密,按理不需要规定有效期限,一旦影响国家安全的理由消失,应使保密命令失效。但不订期限的保密命令,对发明人权益影响很大,因为发明人根本无从对其发明的实施运用做出相关规划。因此，对于保密命令期限问题，有人主张应该搭配更严谨的审核标准、更完善的援助制度等配套措施，不制定保密命令有效期限，或甚至订为永久保密，以此明确告知发明人没有取得专利权的可能，以便利用类似转让或卖断给政府的方式，取得合理金额的补偿。这种做法较符合法律精神，也减轻了行政机关逐年审查的工作负荷。

（2）专利权年限的延长。美国早期的专利权年限为核发之日起 17 年，因此发明即使被核发保密命令，仍能在保密命令废止后按照专利实际核发日期享有完整的专利权期限；但在新的专利法依据 GATT 的相关规定修正后，专利权期间已修改为自申请日起算 20 年，因此，发明人提出专利申请而接到保密命令，将影响完整的专利权期间的实施运用权益，故美国专利法允许依保密期限延长专利权年限，但不得超过 5 年。但"5 年"的标准从何而来，国会立法时并无相关的解释，对于保密期限超过 5 年的，其发明人的权益仍然受到损害，且无特定的援助措施。因此，对于因保密命令可延长不超过 5 年的专利年限，也有进一步检讨的必要。

（3）处罚条款。处罚条款中对违反保密规定的发明人的处罚方式包括放弃专利权、罚金及拘禁，遭到处罚过度的质疑。民众认为，处罚必须视保密命令制度是否符合宪法以及立法目的而定。

3. 发明人是否有足够的选择可以对保密命令提出援助要求。

（1）援助制度的合理性。发明者对保密命令提出异议的渠道有三：主管的行政机关、专利局、商务部长。向商务部长提出异议申诉是最重要的渠道，因为商务部长未涉入先前核发保密命令的程序。但从法律条文及美国行政程序法的规定，对于无法核发的专利权，发明人难以寻求"司法审查"（judicial review）的帮助。

（2）补偿制度的合理性。法律条文规定补偿的范围包括"保密命令造成的损害"和"政府利用该发明"两部分。事实上从 1945

年到 1979 年，国防部受理申请补偿的案件共计 29 件，只有 9 件获得补偿，国防部武装服务专利委员会（Armed Services Patent Advisory Board，ASPAB）平均每核发 1 000 件保密命令，只有 1 件申请补偿，显示发明人接到保密命令想要取得补偿的困难度很高，主要有两个原因：(a) 难以举证证明确实遭受损害；(b) 行政机关拥有补偿与否及补偿金额的行政裁决权。当发明人的补偿申请被驳回后，只好寻求司法审查程序，依据判例法（case law），法院往往依据财产权，认为只要发明人拥有该发明的所有权，政府要求保密却拒绝补偿是不合理的。因此，当发明人对于请求补偿金无法从行政援助的渠道获得满足，只好再诉诸较昂贵、复杂的司法程序。因此，民众希望专利保密制度也能像《原子能法》（Atomic Energy Act of 1954）那样建立一套公正客观的补偿金计算标准，同时核发保密命令和受理申请补偿案件应由不同行政机关办理。

（二）政府要求科技信息保密的争议

1. 9·11 事件以后紧缩管制的争议。美国积极推动科技创新研究与技术转移法制，但前提是必须兼顾国家安全，因此，在《拜杜法案》、EO128295 的《国家产业安全计划》中，均曾提及保密方面的要求，但都仅是提示性的条文，在实际执行时，仍需回归 EO12598 的国家机密保护系统和针对科技信息披露所制定的 NSDD-189 规范中。1985 年里根政府制定的 NSDD-189，是基于维护国家安全目的的，但仍肯定了维持校园研究开放性的必要性，要求尽最大程度维护基础研究不受限制，也无须管制成果发表；只有在政府资助大学的研究计划中，在国家安全的相关配套措施下，某些科技成果或信息必须为机密。因此，这个命令受到各大学普遍的支持，至今仍在有效实施中。

可见，以往美国政府与民间科技研究单位有一定共识，"基础研究"不会受到政府管制或要求保密，只有属于应用性的科技，在不当利用可能影响国家安全时，才会受到管制。但是9·11事件以后政府对学术界增加的一些限制，尤其是管制研究成果发表和外国籍学生参与研究计划的规定，让一些大学感到惊讶和失望。而且同一政府机关委托的两个不同研究项目，也会出现不同的规定条款。为了与政府机构协商或确认这些新增的规定，研究项目的执行时间往往会耽误数个月或超过一年，已有些大学无法接受合约条款新增的限制，而放弃这些研究计划资金。

因此，学术界认为，与以往 EO12598 和 NSDD189 保障基础研究只要不影响国家安全，就不应列入机密的精神相较，现在政府对科技发展的重视程度已逐渐减弱，转而更加重视国家安全。学术界针对科学相对于国家安全如何平衡的议题，提出下列的问题：

（1）对于政府出资研究（包含机关内部及外包的研究）所产生的新管制，对那些政府出资但实际研究内容却是由非政府单位主导执行的研究计划案都要适用？

（2）对 SBU 的管制措施是否适用于核定机密等级和使用机密信息？

（3）计划的保密时长怎么确定？（从预算拨付起？计划开始起？计划完成起？或仅在公开前的审查期间受管制？）

（4）对于非政府人员持有研发信息如何规范？

（5）这些保密措施如何影响政府基础研究的执行？

（6）对于研究成果有持续发展潜能，研究单位有兴趣向产业界争取研究经费的信息如何保密？

（7）研究机构如获得授权可以对原始数据核定机密，这些机构是否也需修正以往鼓励公开发表的政策或规定？

现代科技的发展越来越趋向跨学科的整合与分工，需依赖开放性的研究环境进行沟通交流；基础科学研究成果转移到商业应用的时程越来越短，也使大学、政府研究机构、产业之间更需要开放的

第五章 国防科技保密机制建设争议与问题

沟通交流环境。这使学者疾呼要求维持学术研究环境的"开放性"。在 2002 年 10 月 18 日,国家学术学会(National Academies)的三位主管发表一份有关科技信息交流要寻求安全与开放间平衡的声明文件。文件中指出,为保护策略性秘密,确实有作某些限制的需要,但为了加速科技知识的进步和促进对国家安全威胁的了解,信息的开放也有其必要性。这份文件也要求政府重申"基础科学研究"不应被列为机密,非机密的研究成果信息就不应该管制,而诸如 SBU 等定义不清的分类也不应该使用。经验显示像这种含糊的原则会造成政府官员和科学家在认知上有很大落差,其影响所及必然会扼杀科学家的创造力,进而削弱国家安全能力。该文件也给政府和专业团体提出一些建议,如对保护科技信息的程序展开对话,以制订出有效方法等。

2. 公开前审查的争议。美国联邦政府规定对于那些能接触到机密资料的政府机构现职及离职雇员,或承接政府计划的人员,在欲私人发表科学技术信息时,要接受"公开前审查"(Pre-Publication Review)。例如,农业部在其员工手册中,规定员工公开或发表技术信息前,必须先经过安全审查;又例如国防部在其资助或委托外部研究的契约上,都会有"公开前审查"的条款,规定国防部得对研究信息公开发表前先进行审查。国防部在 2002 年发布的《国防部对研究及技术保护的规定程序》(Mandatory Procedures for Research and Technology Protection Within the DOD)草案,进一步要求研究人员对于军方资助的研究成果,即使不属于机密资料,也必须经过国防部审查同意,才能公开讨论或发表。

美国政府对科技研究成果或信息作"公开前审查",当然与国家机密或敏感性信息保密机制有关,但这种做法显然极不尊重研究单位及研究人员,因此也极有争议。其主要争议点有二:第一,是对于私人所从事的研究开发,是否可以通过权力介入审查或管制,若其科技成果真的含有某些"敏感性"信息，有影响国家安全之虞，政府缺乏整体的政策和法规执行保密或保障人民权益；第二，就是前述已提到的机密与 SBU 的定义不清问题，政府机关根本很难对需要接受审查的人提出明确的审查标准，政府各机关要求的标准也不一致，因此，麻省理工学院（MIT）在最近的一份报告中就拒绝作这种发表前的安全审查。

所以，对于"公开前审查"的做法，有学者建议是在政府资金赞助之前期阶段，就先决定是否要接受发表的管制或保密，这比研究成果完成后要公开发表前才进行审查较不具争议，因为，一般私人赞助的研究合同，也多有对研发成果限制公开的约定。如此研发人员对研究内容的敏感性也有明确的认知，同时也可以在研究合约签订前就协商管制或审查的方法，并可以包含补偿的制度。

反对该制度的人则认为大学等研究机构一般不愿意做研发成果的发表前审查，因此这类措施将限制大学的研究经费来源，同时竞争政府委托研究的研究单位将减少，进而降低研发质量和某些领域的科技发展，此外，计划执行前要判断研发成果是否具有敏感性仍有某种程度的困难，例如，利用白老鼠的繁殖实验来进行物质的毒性测试，若能找到并验证危害人体的物质，可能就需要保密以免被恐怖分子利用，但如果研究结果只是证实该物质不具危害性，则并没有限制发表的必要，这在实验进行前并无法预计研究结果。

三、国际科技保密法制的争议

美国政府对国外的科学技术保密，主要通过科技出口管制制度来实施。对于科技出口管制立法的争议，可以分成两个阵营：一边是为了要促进出口而要求解除管制；另一边则认为解除管制会影响国家安全。这属于政策目的上的争议，与国家机密法制及科学技术保密法制相类似，在此不再赘述。但从操作程序、执行实务及实质

第五章 国防科技保密机制建设争议与问题

影响等角度，还可以对科技出口管制制度做出以下几点探讨。

(一) 科技出口难以有效管制

特定的技术被管制输出到特定国家，但是并无法阻止该国家从其他国家获得该技术。对产业界而言，政府管制的做法，只是将市场机会拱手让给其他有相关技术的国家；尤其现今是产业分工全球化的时代，而政府的科技出口管制制度却仍是根据货物都是在同一国家内制造组装的观念设计，早已不合时宜。所以，从产业界的观点看，会认为军方武器获得方式，已由冷战时期的自行研究开发，转向商业采购行为；而美国企业必须争取国外市场、增加利润，才能再投资研发，维持技术领先优势，这才符合国家安全利益。但反驳这种论点的人则认为将先进技术销售到具有潜在敌意的国家，绝对不会促进国家安全，并以伊拉克在20世纪80年代接受美援却在20世纪90年代以后与美国敌对作为证据。而军方寻求从商业渠道获得武器，是因为国防预算缩减的配套措施，况且军方仍还有预算在从事先进技术发展，绝对有管制的需要。因此，这些站在国家安全立场支持出口管制者，多认为要有效管制技术出口，应在执行面改进，比如说针对进步快速的计算机运算技术检讨管制标准、加强技术输出后使用端的查核等，而不是废除出口管制。

(二) 多边管制协议的有效性

美国参与许多国际间的多边出口管制协议，如瓦圣那协议（WA）、MTCR、NSG等，会员国共同遵守不将某些技术输出到特定国家或区域。这些组织的特征都是有一份共同管制项目清单、定期报告的要求，但也都赋予会员国依其国内法及政策有弹性核准出口的处理权限。产业界非常重视这种多边协议的效力，希望本身因美国国内法而被管制出口的技术，在其他国家的竞争厂商也能受到该国的管制。所以，不论站在产业立场或主张紧缩管制者立场，都希望多边管制的协议能够强化，但仍有一些观察家认为这些协议只是基于各会员国妥协，缺乏足够的执行组织机构和严密的检查机制，基本上缺乏强制效力。

（三）政府核发输出许可程序的争议

美国军民两用货品出口管制是由商务部的产业安全局（Bureau of Industry and Security，简称 BIS）所负责，但是像国防部、能源部、核能规则委员会都介入输出许可的审查，另外，国务院下设有"国防贸易管制办公室"（Office of Defense Trade Controls，简称 ODTC），管制武器和军用技术的输出。对于这样的官僚系统，产业界认为有许多问题：

1. 不同部门间重复审查，对管制物品规格定义也不太一致。
2. 审查至核发许可的时间过长，厂商没法制定制造销售的规划。
3. 许可的标准未能切合技术的优势、管制项目及产业需求。
4. 对于政府不核准输出许可的处分没有司法审查的机会。

至于为政府审查程序辩护者，仍主要以国家安全为挡箭牌，像政府出口管制官员即宣称，考虑审查核对管制清单的项目、检查最终使用者及用途、协调其他相关国家的政府单位等所耗费的时间，其输出许可审查程序仍属透明、公平、迅速的。不过也有主张国家安全的保守派质疑，出口管理业务不应由商务部负责，因为商务部的立场是要照顾产业界利益，很难以国家安全利益为优先。

（四）科技出口管制对美国经济的冲击

科技出口管制制度最受负面的批评就是会影响出口贸易，进而损害美国经济。但不同立场的阵营对统计数字有不同的解读，使其对管制制度所造成经济冲击的程度也就各说各话。因为，单以管制出口所损失的贸易金额计，并不能代表整体经济损失，还必须就进出口究竟属消费品或生产材料、未输出技术是否在国内创造经济效益等许多因素考虑，才能综合分析。一般认为管制出口损失金额的

5%~35%，才是造成整体经济损失的合理金额，但其高低程度的估计仍有极大差距，因此商务部 BIS 在其 2002 年报结论中仍认为出口管制制度对美国经济影响程度不大。

（五）对科技出口管制项目的争议

美国出口管制包含许多"敏感性"科技项目，但这些项目的选定和审查标准有很多争议。例如，计算机软件加密技术有许多商业上的使用，但因为其具有军事上运用的潜能，就被美国政府关注而予管制。而美国业界因不清楚管制的界限和顾虑海外竞争力的因素，就极力对国会及总统游说及施压，因此 1996 年克林顿总统作出软件加密技术允许出口的决定，但也招致政府对敏感性科技管制已经松动的批评。此外，业界也质疑政府彻底管制到软件的原始程序代码（source codes）已违反宪法第一增修条文中的保护言论自由原则。例如，在 Bernstein v. U.S. Dep't of Justice 案中，第九巡回法院审判庭有三位法官认为原始程序代码（source codes）应受宪法第一增修条文的言论自由保护。另一个重要案例是一位法学教授 Peter Junger，他为了课程需要将加密技术的原始程序代码张贴于网站上，同时质疑政府对特定属于加密技术的程序代码进行管制违反宪法的言论自由保护。第六巡回法院同意其观点，认为某些软件原始程序代码确实应受言论自由保护，但法院也认为政府管制软件原始程序代码有其立法上的利益。因此很难就所有案例做成单一结论，还是必须依个案判断原始程序代码是否属于言论自由范围。

所以，对于从事科技产品研发的业者而言，面临许多技术输出管制的潜在风险，因为出口管理规则不仅针对货品出口而已，对各种不同的管制形态也规范甚广，许多业界可能视为例行性的活动都可能不被允许，例如，因特网的使用、研发人员出国研讨交流、国外科技人员来访等，厂商都必须有事前的警觉，额外付出管理成本或事先取得许可，才能避免被处罚。

四、经济间谍法案的争议

（一）立法过程的争议

本书第四章中谈到美国政府以国家安全理由，介入科学技术保密或管制的法律系统，除了国家机密保护、国内科技保密、国外科技保密法制外，还有以商业秘密为保护客体的《经济间谍法案》。由于美国是世界上科技最先进的国家，许多研究成果更是由民间企业所研发拥有，而商业间谍的行为对美国的经济产生极大的负面影响，因此，美国国会于 1996 年举行了一系列的听证会，谋求制定《经济间谍法案》以解决商业间谍的问题。因此，分析其听证会的证词，即可了解制定《经济间谍法案》的需求及理由。当时联邦调查局（FBI）的局长 LouisJ. Free 作证时指出，至少有 23 个国家在美从事商业间谍活动，他并以"美国工业安全协会"（American Society for Industrial Security, ASIS）对于 1992～1995 年情况所作的调查报告为例，指出美国企业遭受知识产权侵害的案件，已经从 1992 年每月平均 9.9 件，增加到 1995 年平均每月 32 件，三年内增加 323 件，而每年所受损害金额则达 2 400 亿美元，这些案件中，60％是战略性计划（Strategic Plans）、研发（R&D）与工艺（Manufacturing Processes）方面的信息，也就是商业秘密法所保护的信息。

美国政府虽然能举出国家利益受到损害的证据，但人民及民意代表对于政府准备大张旗鼓介入民间研发活动，仍有所疑虑。因此美国国会曾举行二次主要的听证会来考虑是否制定联邦法律，以规范及制裁营业秘密窃取行为。这二次听证会的首要证人均为联邦调查局的局长 Louis J. Freeh，由于他指出美国经济以及国家安全已经受到外国商业间谍的威胁，且明确说明美国政府在处理经济间谍行为时的瓶颈与企业需要联邦立法的急迫性，因此美国国会在 1996 年 10 月通过了《经济间谍法案》（The Economic Espionage Act of

第五章 国防科技保密机制建设争议与问题

1996)。从这二次听证会可以归纳出支持该立法的三个主要论点：第一，后冷战时期，美国国内经济发展的重要性与国家安全的重要性，两者不分轩轾；第二，外国力量基于其国内本身产业界的经济利益，通过各种方法积极地向美国政府或公司窃取重要的技术、数据以及信息；第三，美国现行的法律，包括州际传输盗用财产法(Interstate Transportation of Stolen Property Act, 18 U.S.C. Sec.2314)、邮件诈欺（mail fraud）或是通讯诈欺（wire fraud）等，确实无法有效地起诉经济间谍。通过国家安全与经济利益等重大理由，才顺利完成立法。

(二) 刑事责任的争议

美国《经济间谍法案》虽有维护国家安全和经济竞争力的正当目的，但《经济间谍法案》仍是一部非常与众不同的刑事法，它与一般的刑事法相比，其管辖权范围比较广，同时对犯罪的处罚也比较严厉。这主要是因为美国国会希望用该法来打击外国政府所支持的商业间谍活动，并且以政府权力来保护私人企业的商业机密，因而造成某些条款在保障私人的经济利益前提下与一般的刑事法精神大异其趣。所以《经济间谍法案》的矛头是指向国外，其受到最大影响的，并不在于美国人民在司法权益上受到损害，而是外国的政府或企业。也因此，严苛的有期徒刑，与巨额的罚金，是否符合刑事责任的比例原则，应是最大争议所在，但因被起诉的对象，许多是外国人或团体，使这种争议的探讨，在美国相形受到忽视。此外，《经济间谍法案》还规定所有侵害商业秘密的财产或是因犯罪衍生的所得，均得由美国政府没收，此是参酌有关处罚贩毒法规而制定的，其目的是在于被告经济状况不佳时，能够有较广泛的财产可供美国政府没收及拍卖，以赔偿被害人的损害。但这被运用在以商业秘密为客体的案件上，却可能造成被害人的商业秘密已混在被没收的客体中,而遭拍卖的命运;同时,对于没收的界限,《经济间谍法案》并未明确规定,而仅能回归美国宪法第八条的限制,即禁止与犯罪行为显不合比例的没收,但在商业秘密案件上,仍缺乏客观的衡量原则。

(三)刑事程序的争议

再就《经济间谍法案》在刑事程序上来看,也有其缺陷。《经济间谍法案》针对窃取商业秘密,而非针对合法竞争对手,为了避免企业任意陷人于罪,必须证明违犯者有高度的意图(Intent)和对商业秘密作严谨的定义。故美国政府就被告的犯罪事实构成要件,负有"超越合理怀疑"(Beyond Reasonable Doubt)的举证责任。而从证据法的观点,除非有明确的犯罪事证,否则要证明被告有犯罪意图,将十分困难,也因此有美国学者认为因刑事举证责任所造成的障碍,将使得窃取商业秘密能成功定罪的比例降低。事实上,美国联邦调查局探员为取得证据,以假扮的商业秘密卖家"诱陷"外国企业及人士违法的做法,也有争议。

总之,美国《经济间谍法案》是以打击危害国家安全和经济利益的商业间谍行为为主,仍以政府的角度思考,甚于人民在智慧财产上的利益。因为以《经济间谍法案》起诉犯罪行为的,商业秘密所有人虽可利用联邦政府的调查资源,加速保护其免于更大的商业损失,但该窃密案件的所有调查策略、起诉时程、程序等事宜,都由检查机关来决定,商业秘密所有人反而丧失对该商业秘密的处分权,例如,无法与被告成立和解等,都显示《经济间谍法案》重视国家利益甚于人民利益。不过美国政府会采用商业秘密的方式来保护科技研发成果信息,显示商业秘密的保护客体有弥补国家机密保护、限制研发信息公开、科技出口管制等不足之处。

第五章 国防科技保密机制建设争议与问题

第二节

科技保密法制
面临的两难困境

从以上各类法制所产生的争议，可以看出政府基于国家安全理由进行科技成果与信息的保密管制，往往在政策与法制设计上陷入两难的困境（dilemma），因而产生许多法律上的争议点。因此，在整体国防科技保密法制的研究过程中，有必要对这些思想的冲突进行了解与探讨。

一、信息保密 vs. 科技创新

国家的"科学"发展系统和"机密"管理系统，基本上应该是完全相反的思考面向，科学发展需要信息毫无限制的开放和交流，才能使知识流通并促成创意的产生；而机密管理需要对信息作严格的管制才能发挥作为情报的价值。现代国家的科技实力攸关其军事、经济的竞争力，因此，科技发展与国家安全有密切关系，使得"科学"发展和"机密"管理的系统常常牵连在一起。对于科技研究人员而言，希望毫无限制地从其他地方获取各种信息，以解决研究上的问题，但对于所接触或产生的某些信息，也必须有"安全"上的认知，以尽其应有的社会责任。

（一）秘密对科学知识产生的影响

美国学者 Robert K. Merton 认为，"科学"和"秘密"是处于相害、不自然的关系。其采取两段式论点：第一，秘密的科学不能为科学家的发明或发现来作证，或彰显其成就。因此，科学家在从事研究时或许会吝于与他人沟通，但一旦完成研究成果后，就会急于公开发表，因为这牵涉到其学术名声、地位，甚至将来得奖等荣耀。第二，秘密的知识因为没有公开，缺乏充分的讨论和验证，因此造成错误的几率大增。所以 Merton 认为，建立"科学"的基本准则规范是"共有"（communism）、"普遍"（universalism）、"公正无私"（disinterested）、"有系统的怀疑"（organized skepticism），这些准则与"秘密"都不甚相容。

但 Michael Aaron Dennis 则认为 Merton 的说法是属于和平时期科学发展的观点。若回顾战时，尤其像第二次世界战时的"曼哈顿计划"（Manhattan Project），其秘密与科学的关系，就有不一样的观点。美国在第二次世界大战期间秘密执行"曼哈顿计划"研发原子弹，在 1945 年 8 月 5 日之前，只有不到一百人知道计划的全貌。但因为计划能保持秘密，避免不必要的公众讨论的干扰，并保持了军事价值。战后有许多民间的实验室或研究人员也投入军事科技的研发，此时"秘密"和保持秘密的能力，成为民间研究机构争取军方信任的重要因素。此外，不论是否为了战争目的，"秘密"在研发设计过程中也是一个重要元素，研发团队在投入研发之初，若能保持秘密，可以避免无谓的批评、讥讽或反对，直到有初步或稳定的研究成果产生，这对维持研究团队的信心是非常有正面帮助的。以飞机或弹道导弹上的"惯性导引系统"研发为例，其初始的技术构想是要将飞机的加速度和地心重力加速度分离，但这受到当时大多数学者，包括著名的物理学家 George Gamow 的质疑，认为其违反爱因斯坦的相对论；但研发团队只好采取保密的做法，避开外界干扰，直到研发出稳定而有效的产品才对外发表。所以，由此可见研发人员避免在研发过程中对外公开或承诺，使保持类似秘密的状态，是有利于研发计划持续进行的。

第五章 国防科技保密机制建设争议与问题

(二) 秘密对科学技术流通的影响

美国有秘密研发原子弹,取得第二次世界大战决定性胜利的先例,使得多数人较能认同国防科技研发过程中的"秘密"是"必要的恶"。但过度的保密仍会损害科技发展,尤其在科学知识沟通和技术成果交流方面,效果更为明显。MarkFruin 研究 Toshiba 公司的管理发现,Toshiba 在全球许多地方设有工厂,但是对于员工的技能技巧的训练、知识的传递,并不顺利,因为专门技术(know-how)的本质无法包含在手册中,还必须有实务上的练习和经验才能建立。这种沉默的知识(tacit knowledge)不属于秘密,但有类似的效果。信息的管制或秘密会减缓技术的扩散,而沉默的知识因无法顺利传递而一样减缓技术的转移。

因此,科学知识心得的交流和思想创意的沟通,是促成科技研究进步的重要因素。美国大学因为能保持很开放的研究环境,得以吸纳全球各地的优秀学生,汇聚最先进的科学知识,而能维持美国在科技上的领导地位。因此,美国政府在9·11事件后对校园增加的一些限制,尤其是管制研究成果发表和外国籍学生参与研究计划,让学校感到惊讶和失望,使大学校长及教授们疾呼政府应维持校园的开放研究环境。

这些校长或教授们更强调,现今世界上许多重要的科技议题,都有需要寻求全球化解决方案的趋势,例如,针对 SARS(Sever Acute Respiratory Syndrome)的发生,世界卫生组织(WHO)必须发布全球性的警报,并且结合了十个国家的十三个实验室研究 SARS 发生的原因。如果各研究室或各国政府,不能很开放地分享有关 SARS 的疫情、防治、研究成果等各种信息,将使研究进度和研究成果受到很大影响。所以,大学的研究工作必须维持科技上的优势,以实时有效地响应国家的需要,就应该追求开放性、无机密性的研究环境。

所以，在思考政府的科技保密法制上，按照美国学术界一般性的看法，属于基础性研究的信息交流，应尽量不受到干涉，政府介入要求保密，应限于应用性科技，最好局限于政府内部自行研发的部分；同时政府科技保密法制，必须了解以下的一些趋势，而使"秘密"的要求趋于适度及合理，以免妨碍科技发展：

1. 跨学科领域间的科学不断增加：现代科技的发展越来越趋向跨学科的整合与分工，才能获得突破和进步，而传统学科领域间藩篱要被打破，就更仰赖开放性的研究环境进行沟通交流。

2. 科技演变越来越迅速：基础科学研究成果转移落实到民生应用的时程越来越短，新旧科技的取代也越来越快，这都使大学、政府研究机构、产业之间的沟通和交流，更需要开放的环境。

3. 科学研究与教育间必须紧密结合：科学研究与教育间的紧密结合，是美国科技领先的关键因素，因此政府从事科技发展，必须结合教育功能，维持开放性的沟通环境，使学生能毫无阻碍地参加研究团队，发挥创意。

4. 国际间科技交流趋于频繁而密切：政府在科技交流政策上，需保持开放的态度，才能促进国际合作，了解科技新知，使国家的科技发展系统具有敏锐省察力和强大吸收力。

（三）经济分析的观点

专利制度及一般知识产权的基本思考，是为了要保护从事创作发明的思想结晶，赋予发明人以特定权利，但相对也要求将技术内容披露，这是可以兼顾发明人权益及促进整体科技发展的方法。但对于某些发明人或投资从事研发的团体而言，显然将其研发成果隐匿起来，更能具有经济效益。这牵涉到"隐私性"的经济分析，法律经济学大师 Richard A. Posner 即指出："隐私是一种控制和蒙人（misrepresentation），对这种有关隐私的

第五章 国防科技保密机制建设争议与问题

观点的最重要限定涉及观点创新和私人交谈。信息具有公共的特性，这使信息很容易为他人占用。这种占用使这一信息的初始生产者无法补偿他的信息生产投资，因此减少了这种投资的激励。要克服这一问题，与通常理解的市场体制兼容的有两种方法。第一种方法是明确设定信息的产权，就像专利法和著作权法规定的那样。第二种方法是秘密，意思是信息生产者独占使用这一信息，直到他有机会从中获利后才对外泄漏。"

所以，不论是知识产权的创设，或对秘密给予法律保护，都对于科技发展有正面意义。且 Posner 从经济分析的观点，更认为商业信息的隐私，一般说来应当比个人信息的隐私更受保护；因为对于企业家来说，秘密是获取自己创造的社会收益的一种重要手段，但在私人生活中，秘密则可能用来隐藏不那么光彩的事实。而科技研究所需要的保密，正是 Posner 所称的具有社会经济效益的秘密，所以从经济分析的角度，"秘密"对于科技研究开发而言，具有法律上的正当性，这或许可为"科学"与"秘密"的两难困境寻求解决之道。换句话说，利用经济分析的方法，或可从受保护信息的价值、实施信息的费用、信息外泄的风险成本等因素，探讨什么样的保密是社会可欲的，什么样的保密是过度的，而取得较清楚的界限。但此处所提到的隐私利益，仍与个人利益相符，与本书所探讨的可能造成民众权益损害的政府介入科技保密是有所差别的。一般的，政府投入国防预算维持国家安全，已属于经济学上"机会成本"分析的重要课题之一，使政府基于国家安全所制定的科技保密立法的经济分析，不仅包含保密制度本身的效益分析，还必须包含国家安全代价与社会民众损失的平衡问题，是具有复杂因素与背景环境的法律经济分析议题。本书虽未以经济分析为主要立论依据，但认为从经济分析角度，应可再深入探讨，预期对于政府介入科技保密的法律正当性分析，会有所帮助。

二、权威行政 vs. 私权保护

(一) 政府保密法制的权威行政性质

在行政法领域上可以从不同观点将政府行政行为予以分类，其中从适用法规的性质而言，即可大致区分为"权力行政"及"私营经济行政"两大类。权力行政又称权威行政（hoheitliche Verwaltung），为国家或自治团体居于统治权主体的地位，以公法规定为基础所从事的行政行为，是传统行政作用中最主要的一种类型，其重要特征在于行政通常以一般抽象的命令或个别性的处分等方式，要求人民承担一定的义务，必要时得采取强制手段，以达行政目的，在这样的行政作用之下，行政与人民之间形成一种"上下秩序关系"。

若从政府作为的性质或任务而言，政府行政又可分为"干涉行政"、"给付行政"与"计划行政"三类，其中干涉行政（Eingriffsverwaltung）或译为侵害行政，为权力行政中常见的行为方式，指行政机关为达成下命、禁止或确认的效果，所采取的抽象或具体措施，以及必要时所使用的强制手段。

从以上的定义来看，政府介入民间研发活动，实施科技保密制度，是典型的权力行政，也属于干涉行政。权力行政对人民权利造成直接的影响，故需严格遵守依法行政原则的要求，除不得与上述规范相抵触外，尤需有明确的法律授权基础，始得为之，同时也需遵循程序法上的相关法规，不得任意为之；此外，如果权力行政或干涉行政对人民权益产生损害，更应给予行政援助的渠道，以保障人民权益。

因此，政府制定科技保密法制，不能以国家安全为借口而蛮横为之，仍须注重人民权利的保护。尤其现代国家从事科技研究开发，多以"私营经济行政"的方式，委托或补助民间研究机构、企业或大学执行，且民间从事科技研发的比重日益提高，使政府欲介入民间科技研发，要求实施保密，更必须谨慎为之，以免因严重损害人民权益产生争议。

（二）人民财产权的保护

政府实施科技保密措施对人民权利最直接的影响，就是财产权的损害。科技研发成果属于知识产权已毋庸争议，以专利制度而言，专利的第一层重要意义是在于发明人愿意将其发明创作的成果公开出来与大众分享，因此其特性之一是具公开性；而专利的另一层意义，即专利就是政府所赋予的权利，虽为私权利，但这是使发明人愿意将技术内容公开的诱因。因此，政府反过来又要求发明人对涉及国家安全的科技成果保密，不仅有侵害发明人权利之虞，还可能使保密制度产生反效果，发明人因而不愿意从事国防科技研发，或私底下隐藏起来自行实施。

所以，政府在制定科技保密的法制时，必须衡量与人民私权利间的冲突问题。如果保护国家安全利益比保护私人权利对公众有更大利益的话，则政府介入科技保密的立法就较具有正当性。如美国专利保密制度，是起源于战时的需求，但到了和平时期就产生了检讨声音，因为和平时期国家安全所受威胁较小，专利保密制度就应该有更严格的限制，以尽可能保障人民的私权利，包括发明人的财产权和专利制度对公众的利益。所以，政府必须寻求大众对于国家安全有遭到即将或类似的战争威胁的认知，才能正当地介入民间科技保密，否则应该要检讨其条文，适度松绑，包括行政机关核发保密命令的行政裁决权范围，都必须思考检讨调整。

因此，从保护人民财产权的观点看，政府科技保密制度至少应考虑以下的因素，以寻求平衡：

1. 权利归属。例如美国专利法中对于核发保密命令，是依据政府是否已拥有该发明的"财产上的利益"（property interest）来区分。此处"财产上的利益",范围包含其发明所能获得的各项权利的所有权,也就是发明成果的财产权利归属的问题。要衡量该专利发明的"财产上的利益"是否属于政府,美国曾在 1980 年举行听证会定义,即包含"政府雇员代表政府或基于职务责任所产生的发明,由政府申请获得专利相关权利"及"政府契约承包商在契约执行期间所产生的发明"。换言之,在所谓国有(government – owned)或政府控制(government – controlled)的知识产权范围内,其发明申请之财权是政府既有的权利利益,必须依 35USC§181 第一段的规定,经审查后发布保密命令;若未涉及政府既有的财产利益,原则上是归属于民间的发明成果,则依该条文第二、三段的规定审查是否要发布保密命令。

这两者的审查标准及程序是不尽相同的,属于政府财产的研究发明,主要是拥有该发明成果的政府机构,自行认定或相关政府机构主张该发明信息的披露有可能对国家安全产生明显损害,即可由专利局长下令保密;当发明成果为民间私人财产,与政府既有的财产利益无涉时,如通过核发专利公布或披露该发明后,专利局长认为"可能"有害于国家安全时,他应将该专利申请案提供给相关政府机构,其中包括原子能委员会、国防部长,或任何由总统指定为国防单位的部门或单位主管。若审查结果认定"将"有害于国家安全,则原子能委员会、国防部长或指定官员应告知专利局长,而后专利局长下令保持该发明的秘密,并在国家安全的需要下保留该专利权的核发,然后通知该专利申请人。在政府机构提出发布保密命令的要求,而且充分地表达该专利审查可能有害于国家安全后,专利局长应将该申请案保留于密封状况,而后告知申请人该情形。该申请案遭到保密的申请人可在法令许可的范围内向商务部长提出该保密命令的申诉。

由此可知,美国专利申请案不涉及政府的财产利益时,有较严

第五章 国防科技保密机制建设争议与问题

谨的审查程序,第一阶段专利局就必须审查筛选是否可能影响国家安全,第二阶段再交给其他有关的政府机构审查认定。虽然该条文仍未能明确界定审查的标准而有争议,但这种基于财产权归属而所作的区分,显然较能顾及人民财产权的利益;反观中国台湾专利法第五十条的机密专利制度,就未能从发明成果的财产权归属先行区分,政府与民间的研发成果申请专利是用相同的保密审查制度,基本上不利于人民财产权的保护。

2. 援助渠道。从事科技研究因政府科技保密制度而受财产利益损害时,必须提供援助渠道,以恢复其所失利益。例如,美国专利法对于发明者接到保密命令,可以有两个选择:第一,是对保密命令认为错误或过当而提出异议申诉,申诉渠道包括向主管的行政机关、专利局、商务部长提出异议;第二,是依专利法第一百八十三条申请补偿。

美国专利法的补偿机制是允许发明人因为保密命令所致,或是政府征收使用与披露其发明而产生的损害,得请求补偿金。发明人有两种方法寻求补偿金:第一种方法是,可以与当初提出保密需求或使用其发明的政府部门或机构进行协商,该机构首长在接受请求损害赔偿的要求后,有权与发明人达成协议,全部赔偿损害或使用费或偿付使用费并赔偿损失。如果无法达成协议,政府部门或机构的首长可以判定付给发明人一笔款项,其数额不得超过政府部门或机构的首长认为是公平数额的75%。其后损害赔偿请求人可以在联邦法院或请求人居住地的美国地方法院对美国提起诉讼,请求偿付一笔款项,该款项与前述由政府机构首长判定款项加在一起就是对损害或政府使用该发明而构成的合理补偿总额。即使发明人无法从政府部门或机构获得补偿金,仍可以向法院提起寻求补偿的诉讼。第二种方法是,等到保密命令届满,专利核发之后,若没有按前述程序与行政机关达成补偿协议的,可以直接向联邦法院提起请求补偿的诉讼。

对于所谓"合理补偿"(just compensation)的标准，或发明人所遭受损害的合理补偿如何计算，行政机关与法院可能有不同认定。法院一般会依据民事损害赔偿的计算方式，有较周延的认定。例如，因保密命令所致损害，美国法院实务上关于发明人向政府请求补偿金包括：(1) 发明人无法就持续研发所取得的融资或资金损失；(2) 因无法公开其技术上的优越性而丧失潜在使用者或授权机会的权利金损失；(3) 为申诉或申请撤销保密命令所花费的律师等费用，皆可以被认定为请求补偿金的范围，惟原告需作实体上的举证，明确证明有其损失方能计入补偿金的请求金额。若是政府使用其发明，也可利用合理权利金的计算方法决定补偿金额。所以，就单纯被要求保密，或单纯因政府使用，其补偿金的认定大致可采用专利侵权或授权的案例决定，若是含有前文两种状况，则补偿金认定较为复杂，必须就发明人回复其应有权益的可能损害范围，作整体考虑来认定。

所以，美国专利法规与法院实务已对被要求保密的发明人提供异议及补偿的援助渠道，但发明人对于无法被核发专利权，尚无寻求"司法审查"的途径，而仍受批评。也就是说，发明人收到保密命令，经向行政机关异议无效后，又不想经过冗长司法程序才能获得损害填补，而想直接寻求保密命令的司法审查，希能获得裁定必须核发专利权，法院基本上是不会受理的。这在重视私权保护的人士眼中，仍是制度上的重要缺陷。因此，从人民财产权的观点，行政及司法的援助渠道必须合理考虑。

(三) 立法规定政府介入权的，除了科技成果保密外，还有科技成果运用方面，"介入权"(march–in right)行使对人民拥有研发成果的知识产权，有类似的损害情况。政府对于民间研发成果运用的介入权，一般的可包括"强制授权"与"收归国有"两种权力

第五章　国防科技保密机制建设争议与问题

"强制授权"（日本专利法称"特许实施"）是国际间专利制度已通用实行的措施之一，因为专利制度的目的在于促进技术的进步，及确保发明的实施利用，若发明人取得专利后，却不进行实质利用，则法律并无保障其独占使用的必要。尤其发明成果具有公共性或公益性时，权利人的消极不作为而未能发挥其功能效益时，政府有权行使介入权授权第三人实施，以增进公益。目前为了使卫生条件落后的国家地区改善人民健康情形，能够以低廉的价格获得具有专利权的药物，"强制授权"更成为国际间知识产权的重要议题。

"收归国有"则属于强制征收的行政行为，专利保密制度就常包含征收手段，如我国国防专利制度。但收归国有的目的不仅为了保密，还可以包括基于政府目的的实施运用。

现代国家除了知识产权法规外，为了推动政府出资的研发成果运用，在相关的技术转移法制上，也明订介入权行使的要件与程序。例如，美国《拜杜法案》为确保政府资助的研发成果有效实施，及保障国家与公众利益，在特殊情况下，政府于必要时得行使介入权，以非专属授权、部分专属授权或专属授权的方式，强制授权予第三人实施，无须取得权利人同意。而政府行使介入权的要件，可以简单归纳为"确保研发成果应用"、"维护公共利益与公众卫生"及"美国工业优先"三者。而程序上也规定政府有发动介入权的事实与必要时，原则上应先以非正式方式进行听证程序，并就事实内容加以调查；在完成非正式听证后，政府资助机关应以书面通知受资助机构与其受让人或专属被授权人，对于行使介入权决定有所不服时，可于60日内向联邦上诉法院提起诉讼以资援助。

日本仿效美国《拜杜法案》于1999年制定《产业活力再生特别措施法》，虽未明确规范政府行使介入权的具体要件及进行介入的程序，但该法第三十条规定，接受政府委托计划的受托机构或企业，欲取得研发成果所有权或专属授权时，必须同意日本政府得依公益需要取得无偿使用权；以及受托机构在一定期间内无正当理由为运用该成果时，政府得强制授权予第三人。而该条文对于政府行使介入权的规定，其性质原则上仅为政府为让与或授权该受托机关的法定要约，因此应订于契约条款，契约内容需包含政府行使介入权的程序与援助程序等。所以，该要约尚需经过受托机构或企业的承诺后，其让与或授权契约才算正式成立，一旦政府行使介入权产生争议时，则可由法院依据契约内容以及相关事实做成判断，解决纷争。

由此可知，政府对于研发成果所有权已由受资助机构取得后，再行使介入权可能对权利人造成利益上损害，因此，在立法制度上必须谨慎为之，对行使要件、程序及援助渠道必须预先设想。反观科技保密制度，以"国家安全"作为前提，对于人民研发成果的权利造成更大范围及更严重的影响，政府依比例原则对于实施保密的要件、程序，理应在法制上有更详细而明确的陈述，并提供更充分的援助渠道，以维护人民权益。

三、保密管制 vs. 言论自由

从人民基本权的角度出发，除了财产权之外，还包括个人自由相关的权利。从美国政府执行的科技保密制度，包括论文发表前的审查，可知保密管制的范围，不仅针对已取得明确权利范围的科技研究成果，尚且涵盖与研发活动有关的信息，因此对人民在言论自由方面的基本权产生冲突。

（一）"言论自由"的意义与范围

从近代民主立宪国家基本权的发展过程观察，人民争取基本权的目的无非在争取作为一个人的尊严，而人性尊严的基本内涵包括"人的主体性"和"人的自由意志"。在体现人的主体性方面，就是不可以将人当作是一个客体或一项工具加以使用，因此，人生而平

第五章 国防科技保密机制建设争议与问题

等,并享有工作权、财产权等,保障人作为法律上的权利义务主体;在自由意志方面,是因为人有自由意志,才能针对各种相关情况作理性分析,为自己行为负责,使人实际上可以作为各种权利义务的主体。因此,美国在 1776 年的维吉尼亚权利法案(Bill of Rights Virginia),可说是美国第一部成文宪法,即宣示:"人生而为自由、独立,并拥有不可让渡的权利";1789 年的宪法增修条文更列举了重要的基本人权,如信仰自由、言论自由、出版自由、请愿权、集会自由、一事不二罚、禁止征收等。所以,"言论自由"作为宪法上所保障的基本权,已为现代民主法治国家所接受。

言论自由是指人民以语言或其他足以表达其思想内容的媒介,如文字、图画、声音以表达出个人的价值判断或转述事实的自由。广义的言论自由,除言论、讲学、著作及出版自由外,还应包括通讯、集会、结社及其他各类形式的言论自由,国内学者为避免混淆,有用"表现意见的自由"、"表现自由"或"意见自由"等词来指称广义的言论自由。本项所探讨的政府对于科技信息的保密管制措施与言论自由的冲突,也指广义的言论自由。

言论自由虽已被普遍接受为自由民主社会不可或缺的基本人权,但宪法保障言论自由程度为何,应该以什么标准来界定言论自由保障的范围,却众说纷纭,即便保障言论自由最力的美国,其法院判决及学说理论对于言论自由的价值为何,也没有共同一致的见解。有国内学者整理美国关于言论自由保障目的与价值的学说探讨,大致上可分为以下三种理论:

1. 追求真理说(truth - seeking theory),或称为言论自由市场说(theory of marketplace of ideas)。

2. 健全民主程序说(democratic; process theory)。

3. 表现自由说(self - expression theory),或称为实现自我说(self - fulfillment or self - realization theory)。

(二)"言论自由"与政府管制

由上述三种不同的言论自由理论所界定出的言论自由范围也不一致。事实上以社会大众的利益为由,即使现代民主国家的政府也常常有干涉言论自由的措施,对于"新闻自由"的管制就是一个例子。新闻自由与言论自由都是保障意见的表达,因此在具体个案上,对于新闻自由与言论自由的界限,所发展出来的一些判断标准或原则,通常是可以通用的;但新闻媒体具有监督政府的功能,因此对于宪法为何保障新闻自由的理论,除了言论自由的理由外,美国额外发展出"第四权理论"。

无论如何,新闻自由较单纯的言论自由有更大的影响力,包括正面的信息传播能力和负面的煽动力量,使得政府常有理由对新闻媒体伸出干涉之手。例如,美国 1934 年的《通讯法案》(Communications Act of 1934)及其后的修正条文规定,美国联邦通讯委员会(Federal Communication Commission)在核发广播电视执照时,必须基于"公众的便利、利益及需要"的考虑,而政府对电子媒体传送信息的电波频率等资源加以统筹分配,都具有管理与管制的性质。美国在 1971 年发生著名的"五角大楼文件案"(the Pentagon Paper)中,联邦最高法院也承认,政府若有足够证据证明文件信息的披露会对国家安全造成重大危害,则事前限制行为并不违宪。

所以,政府对新闻媒体实施的管制措施,一般已被认为是一项具体且重要的公共行政项目,只是在管制的目的及手段上,必须不违反新闻自由理念。纯粹以言论自由为出发点,则政府管制手段应限于程序性或结构性管制手段,也就是不涉及言论或表意内容的管制措施;但大多数情况是,政府顾虑国家安全、社会风气等诸多因素,仍有可能对新闻报道内容采取强硬的控制措施。

言论自由或新闻自由可能对国家安全造成影响,最常见的探讨莫过于煽动内乱行为的言论,是否受言论自由的保障?美国在1919年由Oliver Wendell Holmes, Jr.大法官,在Schench案中即提出"明显而立即危险"(clear and present danger test)作为解决煽动内乱行为言论是否受到宪法保障的判定标准,后经法院、学理的反复的争辩,在1969年的Brandenburg v. Ohio案中,法院提出修正的明显而立即危险原则后,即成为法界与学界趋于一致的共识。依据这项原则,抽象性的煽动言论或报道尚受到宪法言论自由的保障,除非涉及的言论会对暴力革命的发生具有"明显而立即的危险",包括能举证证明:

1. 表意人有煽动他人立即以暴力为政治或社会变革行为的故意。

2. 表意人的言论依其正常合理的用法,可以理解为就是要煽动或产生立即发生暴力的政治或社会变革行为。

3. 根据客观环境判断,表意人的言论确有引致立即发生暴力的政治或社会变革行为的可能性。

此外,基于社会公益的考虑,有些言论及出版品也被排除在言论自由范围之外。从美国最高法院的判决中,可以发现美国宪法第一增修条文是不保障猥亵(obscenity)、儿童色情(child pornography)等方面的言论,而对于商业性、毁谤性、有害于儿童及广播电视上的言论也不完全保障。

由此可知,政府基于国家安全或公众利益而管制新闻媒体,虽具有正当性,但在管制内容及手段上仍必须非常严谨,才能维护民众在言论自由方面的基本权。

(三)从言论自由观点探讨政府科技保密措施应有的限制

政府对科技信息或成果的公开发表,进行限制或管制,多谓是基于国家安全理由,实与管制新闻自由有异曲同工之妙。但政府对于科技资讯的保密措施,并未如新闻自由的管制受到普遍的关注与

重视,本书认为主要理由大略为:

1. 科技研发的信息涉及艰深的专业知识,并非一般民众有能力或有兴趣知悉的东西。

2. 科技信息的发表多限于特定场合或刊物,如学术研讨会或论文期刊,知悉的人士相对是属于少数民众。

3. 一般民众缺乏专业上的知识与程度,去评论国家基于安全理由管制科技信息的措施是否合理。也因为这些理由,将更难以判断政府的科技保密措施能比新闻媒体管制措施取得更高的正当性。事实上,科学家愿意将研发信息及成果公开,主要是基于成果推广运用可取得财产上的利益,或是与相关领域科学家交流以寻求突破及争取学术声望,应享有言论上的自由;且科学技术的发表到被应用常需要一段时间,科学家若真有危害国家安全的故意或意图,如何证明其有危害国家安全的意图?

所以,从言论自由的观点看,若运用类似"明显而立即危险"的原则来审查,政府限制科技信息发表的措施恐失去正当性,有违反宪法保障人民基本权之虞。因此,就习惯法国家而言,仍有发展审查政府"科技保密"措施是否违宪的理论与原则的空间;就成文法国家而言,政府的"科技保密"制度,必须合乎宪法原理,即对于人民基本权利限制必须遵守"法律保留原则"、"比例原则"立法建构,才能避免争议及对人民权利的损害。

四、国家机密保护 vs. 政府信息公开

就所保护的法律利益而言,国家机密保护与政府信息公开是属于相互对立的法制,本书在第四章第二节中已述及美国对敏感性但非属机密(SBU)信息管制与其《信息自由法案》(FOIA)的冲突,就是属于此类争议。科技研发信息,往往更难界定是属于国家机密,或是属于为了科技发展而应该公开交流的信息;尤其政府耗费

人民纳税钱所投入的研发，基于政府信息公开的精神，人民有知情的权利，其对于政府科技保密法制的设计，实有深入思考的必要。

（一）国家机密的定义与范围

从比较法的角度观察，各国立法例对于"国家机密"的概念，并没有一致性的定义。各国对于"国家机密"的内涵，在规范上采取定义的方式，大致有以下三种：

1．"形式定义"，即在文本中明确规定国家机密的内涵与类型，例如英美法国家对于国家机密即采取分类列举方式。

2．"实质定义"，即对于国家机密法权益的保护，设定处罚规定，但是在构成要件的规定中，对于侵害客体的具体涵义及范围，却未加以规定，容许法官在适用法律时，以解释及自由裁量的方式加以衡定。

3．"基本概念的规范"，属于前两者的折衷形式，其特色在于基本的重要法益保护条文上，就国家机密的概念设定规范的准则，诸如机密的客体、范畴、保密要件及一般公开性信息界限等，但其具体规范的构成要件要素，仍保留给法官，依据解释法律的理论加以裁量。对于成文法类型国家，基于罪刑法定主义，又难以客观具体描述国家机密的性质及违反的构成要件，多采取第二及第三种方式规范。

所以，国家机密的内涵与范围并不容易定义。如果采取形式定义，还可以列举出一些类型，如美国总统12958号行政命令所列举7种机密信息的类型，其中一项为"与国家安全有关的科学、技术或经济事务"，因此可以涵盖科学技术信息。但是这样的定义仍然过于笼统，科学技术信息的特性是，非有该领域的专长背景的人，无法确切了解该信息的用途及其可能造成的危害性，然而具有核定机密权限的人，未必是熟悉该技术领域的专家，因此，做出不合理判断的机会远较其他类别的信息来得高。

国家机密法制，应着重在公共部门的秘密保护，包括规范政府对于机密信息的核定、保管、持有的程序与处理方式，其立法目的之一是要排除政府对于私领域信息的干预，保障人民权益，则对于科技信息保密而言，显然无法管辖到民间研发的部分；且国家机密的违反，均负有极大的刑事责任，这对没有危害国家意图、单纯从事研发的科技人员而言，真是难以承受之重。因此国家机密法制，可以将科技信息纳入国家机密范围，但不能完全涵盖科技保密需求。有关科学技术的信息或文件，被核定为机密，或被盖上机密标示，当然就纳入国家机密的管制系统运作；但从科技保密的角度，有两方面是需要思考的：第一，既有的国家机密系统对于机密的审查，是否有足够能力对科技方面的信息加以认定；第二，在国家机密系统之外，显然还需要其他措施，搭配行政法及民法的设计，才能较好地达成科技保密的目的。

（二）政府信息公开的目的与范围

现代化民主国家的人民，对于政府信息公开的要求，主要是防止政府垄断行政信息，使正确舆论难以形成，无法对政府行政有效监督；个人权益有所损害时，也难以迅速获知及反应。就国家主体而言，现代民主国家基于民主原则，强调国家主权属于人民，则政府所拥有的信息，当然属于人民。所以，政府信息公开的目的就是要求政府将拥有的信息主动、适度公开，实现国民主权与民主原则，满足人民"知情权"（right to know），并藉此能适度监督政府、促进行政程序的公开化与透明化。

对于政府信息公开的观念及法制，美国一向是最具代表性的，因为美国早在1966年即已制定《信息自由法案》（FOIA），确立任何人皆有向行政机关请求信息的权利。美国《信息自由法案》规定，除非在法定例外情况下，政府信息原则上均需强制公开，其立法目的是在于确保人民能便于取得及拥有充分行政机关的信息，实

第五章 国防科技保密机制建设争议与问题

现公开政府的目标，构成民主社会监督政府的基础。

美国《信息自由法案》施行以来，实务上最主要的争议之一，就是政府应公开披露的信息范围到底有多广的问题。该法案中有9种免于强制公开的例外规定，但是其中除了依法律所指定形态的记录或信息外，其他8种类型的信息，行政机关仍然保有决定是否披露的权力。这种适用范围上的争议，堪称是 FOIA 的"核心目的"的争议，美国实务判决上，就常对该法案的核心目的究竟为何，进行论述或辩论。此外，在今天信息科技高度发展的时代中，政府掌握的信息日益增多，社会运作及民众对信息需求更趋复杂，原来1966年所制定的法案在政府提供信息的程序及做法上也已不符民众需求，因此美国在1996年进行修法，通过所谓《电子信息自由法》（Electronic Freedom of Information Act，简称 E - FOIA），即针对核心目的争议的澄清及信息电子化需求，对原来的 FOIA 进行修正；虽然 E - FOIA 往往被认为是美国信息自由法制迎头赶上数字化时代的重要成就，但究其实际，仍不能完全解决民众请求信息权利范围的所有问题。

除美国外，欧盟理事会也采取北美法"信息自由"的观念，于1990年6月7日发布《自由接近环境信息理事会准则》，规定会员国有制定环境信息接近权的法律义务，其目标主要有二：一是使任何人享有自由接近信息的权利；二是向会员国提出了推动信息政策的义务。因此，如德国原本在信息公开法制及理论发展较为保守与缓慢，但受到欧盟法制影响，也于1994年制定《环境信息法》，该法规定任何人皆享有信息请求权，但也有一些排除规定，主要是基于公共利益的保护（第七条）与私人利益的保护（第八条）两项理由。基于公共利益方面，对于信息请求权定有"排除"（Auschluβ）与"限制"（Beschränkung）的规定，其可以排除的原因包括：（1）保护国家利益；（2）避免影响司法程序进行；（3）防止危害环境利益；（4）防止权利滥用；（5）涉及来自第三人所提供的信息。而在基于私人权益保护方面，则针对：（1）保护与个人有关的资料；（2）保护知识产权；（3）保护商业秘密等。三项设有对信息取得权的排除规定。

同属成文法体系的日本，于1999年制定《行政机关信息公开法》，2000年发布《行政机关信息公开法施行细则》，并于2001年4月1日施行；该法以政府保有信息的公开为原则，不公开为例外，对于不公开的信息，包括：（1）为保护隐私的个人信息；（2）法人或团体需要保密的信息；（3）与国家安全及公共安全相关信息；（4）审议或检讨中的信息；（5）公开可能导致妨害的行政机关事务或经营的事业有关信息。

从这些法制先进国家的立法例，可以了解行政信息公开已为政府不可避免的趋势，但在法制上仍可以对某些可以免除公开的信息，做出豁免规定，但各国在豁免范围大小上的规定差异很大。

（三）国家机密与信息公开对于科技保密的意义

对于现代化国家而言，国家机密保护与政府信息公开，都是属于有明文规范的法制，且基本上具有对立与互斥的性质，因此，在立法过程中也常相互探讨以寻求平衡。但国家机密对于政府信息而言，只是可以免于公开信息的其中一项，并非互补性的规定。换句话说，既然可以将那些有可能影响国家安全的科技研发信息排除到信息公开范畴之外，就可以直接将其定义为国家机密，这样就无需另行探讨科技保密的问题了；但实际的情况并非如此，因为能基于国家安全理由被排除于信息公开之外的信息，并无法完全属于国家机密。国家机密的保护，属于干涉行政，机密的核定必须有严谨的程序，违反而泄密者有严重的刑责；但反观行政信息公开法律，是对政府要求义务的法制，而国家安全是可以免除信息公开义务的正当理由，因此拥有此项行政裁决权的政府机关，无须将国家机密与信息公开的标准有任何连结,因此在国家机密及必须公开的信息中,仍存在一个模糊区域。而国防科技研发信息,正是处于该模糊地带的代表性信息之一,因为国防科技研发,是可以同时增进国防、科技、经济发展的行为;国防科技研发信息,则涵盖基础性、学术性、应用性的科学知识,若草率认定为国家机密,将损害科技经济的发展,若放任而完全予以公开,又可能为有心人士或敌人利用来危害国家安全。

所以,从政府信息公开或国家机密法制的角度来看,并无法完全涵盖科技信息的管理需求。因为以科技研发信息的效果而言,明显具有危害国家安全性质的,自应列入国家机密;至于只是对国家安全有潜在影响的,基本上可运用信息公开法规的排除条款,免于强制公开,但所谓敏感性信息或潜在影响的认定不易,且政府不公开不代表具有保密效果。再以科技研发信息的归属而言,政府信息公开或国家机密法制都应局限于政府所拥有的信息为范围,民间所产出或拥有的科技研发信息就不受管辖。所以探讨信息公开及国家机密法制与法理,对于科技研发信息保密上的意义,并不在于该两种法制所产生的冲突,而是发现在该两种法制之外,确实存在一个空间必须针对科技保密需求制定规范。

第三节 科技保密法制

科技保密法制的设计,应先就所规范的法律行为主体及客体予以厘清。科技保密的主体,包括执行研发者、拥有研发成果者、接受技术转移者、或接触研发信息的人,视保密的范围、强度、目的等因素承担不同程度的保密义务。因此，运用民法上的观念，以能享有权利、负担义务的权利主体，即自然人与法人，作为科技保密法制上的行为主体，尚无疑义；但在保密客体方面，因为科技研发的特性使然，难以下明确的定义，因此值得探讨。

一、科技研发成果的定义

科技研发成果的表现，并不一定产生有形的物品或硬件，有时是以非特定的信息状态呈现，如技术数据、图纸、磁盘、光盘、程序等，甚至可以无形地储存于人的大脑中。即使一项科技研发成果的最终表现是一种新的硬设备时，其研发成果的全部价值，并不是指科研成果得以寄托的硬设备本身，而是在于它通过研究开发活动解决了特定的技术问题，并获得解决问题的设计、制造技术及知识、经验。以下将从几个不同面向，观察科技研发成果所具有的特征。

1. 科技研发成果在"内容"上具有知识性及创造性的特征，任何技术发明都凝结着一定的科学知识和技能，产生于发明者创造性的脑力劳动过程之中，通常不具有固定形体，因此无法属于民法上的特定物，以种类物描述的也嫌不精确。

2. 科技研发成果在"所有权"的问题上无法以有形物质代表的，因此多仅能以具有财产权视之，但研发成果仍具有"一次产出、多次转让、多方使用"的特征，与一般民法上的动产、不动产有所差异。

3. 即使研发成果的所有权获得厘清，但在其"使用、收益、处分"等方面，仍是以一系列的消化、吸收的连续实施过程，为其特征，并无法以传统物权上银货两讫的观念看待。

4. 科技研发成果在"价值"上也具有难以客观鉴定，且随时间推移，易因技术知识普及或被取代，致使价值巨幅损耗的特征。

第五章 国防科技保密机制建设争议与问题

因为科技研发成果具有这些复杂特征,因此难以使用文字作明确定义。美国在繁复的科技保密及管制规定中也没有对科学技术成果的定义,有统一性的明文叙述。以科技出口管制为例,技术项目涵盖其相关技术数据均为受管制对象,但在相关规范中对"技术"(Technology)及"技术数据"(Technical data)的定义并不尽一致,如表5-1:

表5-1　　　　　　技术与技术数据定义表

规范名称	定　义
国防部"军事关键技术清单"（Militarily Critical Technologies List，MCTL）	技术（Technology）:"产品开发、制造或使用所需的特定信息和专门知识,包括达此目的所需的硬件与软件" 技术数据（Technical data）:"可能表现的形态如蓝图、计划、图形、模型、方程式、表格、工程设计和规格、手册和指示文件是以书面记载或由其他媒体或装置所纪录的,诸如盘片、磁带仅供读取的内存等。"
"出口管理规则"（Export Administration Regulations，EAR）	技术数据（Technical data）:"可以被使用或运用在物品或材料的设计、生产、制造、利用、重建等任何形态的信息。这些数据可以是有形的,如模型、原型、蓝图、或操作模型;或是无形的,如技术服务等。"

技术数据（Technical data）（International Traffic in Arms Regulations，ITAR）:"与国防物品直接有关的设计、工程、发展、生产、处理程序、制造、使用、操作、拆检、修理、维修、改良或重建的信息。包括下列例示形式的信息:蓝图、草图、照片、计划、指令、计算机软件和文件等。也包括可以增进美国军火清单所列项目的技艺状态的信息,但不包括一般性科学、数学或工程原理的信息。"

技术数据（Technical data）由 ITAR 与 EAR 所规范《国家产业安全计划作业手册》（National Industrial Security Program Operating 的信息。具有军事性质的技术资料出口受 ITAR（22 CFR 120.1 -

130.17，1987）管制。兼具军事及民生用途的（Manual，NISPOM）技术资料出口受 EAR（15 CFR 368.1–399.2，1987）管制。

同时，也有美国学者对于技术知识（technical knowledge）区分出不同的类型，从公开传递知识的教科书，到附着于人身上的沉默知识，具有不同的特征（见表5-2）：

表5-2　　　　　　　　技术知识特征表

类　型	特　征
教科书和参考书、专书、评论报告、手册、期刊、研讨会论文集、专利	"玻璃箱"性质：透明，容易取得。不论来源如何，多以文字写就。多数是定量的，以数学模型、算法、经验结果为依据，在参考文献等方面的质量控制良好。
未出版的技术报告（会议论文、政府报告、学术和培训的讲义、公司内部报告、咨询报告）	灰色地带的文献；分散的、难以找到；一般都不通过出版商、书店、图书馆来提供；对民众限制或保密；可能只有外语本；很少或毫无审查其正确性可能不完整或在使用时还必须仰赖其他。
贸易与商业的出版物、计算机程序与文件、物理与数学模型、计算机数据库、军用标准和工业标准、军用设计手册、工程图纸、蓝图、材料清单、程序单、说明书和修理手册	通常是专有财产。
实验方法和技术能量	有些整理的很好（如专业机构或行业协会认可的标准试验方法），另外有一些是经验和沉默的知识，其质量管理试验的方法可能是专有财产。
日常性工作、公司的业务操作和训练手册	可以附着在人身上（不明显）；有时只能通过个人的经验来学习和传授。
对国防部和其他合约所做的投标案和提案	一般是机密的。
商业秘密	在定义上属于专有财产。
沉默的知识（根据经验判断、启发和直觉），通过个人或有组织地进行	"黑箱"性质：难以精确说明；通常很难解释；通常是不定量的。

所以,一般在法制上要对研发成果信息作明确定义及范围界定是有困难的,这使研发人员易于忽略手上所拥有或经手过的一些数据、信息也属于保密标的,造成科技保密系统的漏洞。依本书见解,要能较完整涵盖科技研发成果的范围,应包含下列各项:

1. 各种有形的研发成品:最易令人理解的研发成果,就是能表现研发目的及功能的有形对象,例如武器系统、机器设备、雏形品(prototype)、模型、零组件、设计蓝图、药品等。

2. 各种配方:通常是材料、药品、试剂、食品、化学品等,虽然一般可以通过分析了解其构成元素,但大多无法还原成目标产品。所以配方是含有一定成分比例的物质(包含混合物),并可能包含其制作程序与方法。

3. 各种方法:并非指一般习知技术,而是完成该研究成果的特定方法,包括设计、生产、制造、试验、检测、验证、控制、调节、调度、使用、计量等方法,也可以包括各种管理、组织、指挥、规划、计划等方法。

4. 各种工艺:并非指一般常规性的工艺,而是通过该研究成果的完成,所建立的各种特定的技巧、技能或技艺等。

5. 各种专用装置:新科学成品的研发、测试、产制,一般必须先设计特殊的工具、设备或装置等,包括各种模具、夹具、型架、仪器、装置等。

6. 各种经验的总结:通过研发、测试、产制等过程,所累积的各种技术经验,包括内部标准、准则、规定、经验公式、技术参数、技术诀窍等。

7. 各种计算机软硬件的程序或电路布局:随着信息科技的发展,计算机设备的运用日益广泛,并不断产生新形态的应用方式。为了特定研发目的,所开发完成的软件及其程序代码(source code)、集成电路布局、逻辑控制程序等,若无法归类于前述六项的，仍应视为研究成果。

8. 各种记录或描写前述 7 项信息的文件或媒体：例如设计草图、研究纪录簿、论文、手册、文件、磁盘、光盘、影带等各种载体。

二、秘密种类的分析及国防科技秘密定义探讨

前项所述的 8 种形态科技研发成果信息，都可能有保密需求，需要保密的拟简称为"科技秘密"。构成"科技秘密"的原因和目的有各种可能，例如研发人员为避免干扰而自行保密；本书所讨论的范围，是针对政府基于国家安全需要，对与军事运用有关的科研成果，需要加以管理及保密的，故拟称之为"国防科技秘密"。当然政府基于其他特定目的，如社会公益、科技经济发展等需要，也有可能介入科技研发成果保密，其或可称之为"国家科技秘密"，但其仅是范围上的不同，保密管制方法及手段应近似，因此本书以"国防科技秘密"作为代表，探讨法制建立和保密管制的方法，如要适用到"国家科技秘密"，则在范围上扩张即可。

所谓"科技秘密"或"国防科技秘密"，并非法律上的专有名词或惯用语，本书先前已介绍的相关法制，所产出的秘密名称，包括"国家机密"、"秘密专利"、"商业秘密"等，都与"科技秘密"或"国防科技秘密"的形式或定义有所差异。

"国家机密"是由政府权责主管核定而产生，一般而言属于有形成品的研发成果、依规定必须呈核的文件等，易于管制及核定为国家机密；但前文科技研发成果形态中，有些属于方法、工艺、经验，是附着于人身上的技能或知识，恐怕无法以核定机密的方式保密，而科技研发成果数据繁复，权责主管通常也无法巨细靡遗地了解其机密性，研发人员为贪图研发工作的便利性，也不会主动提报为机密，因此"国防科技秘密"显然无法仅以国家机密的方式达到

第五章　国防科技保密机制建设争议与问题

周延的保密。

"秘密专利"是建构于专利审查系统中的产物，必须由发明人主动提出专利申请，政府才有机会介入审查和要求保密。对于有心逃避国家审查的，或基于其他理由不愿申请专利的，政府并无介入的机会，因此专利保密制度对于"科技秘密"或"国防科技秘密"的保护也有时而穷。

至于"商业秘密"，一般是属于私法性质的法律，由民间企业或研究单位自行认定管理，有争议时再循司法渠道解决，基本上行政机关无由介入，与本书所探讨政府对"科技秘密"或"国防科技秘密"执行保密的目的不同。但是，商业秘密在定义方式及执行保密的方法、精神上，却相当能考虑到"科技保密"的需求，是值得政府在建立"科技秘密"或"国防科技秘密"的保密系统上作为参考的（见表5-3）。

表5-3　　　　　　　　规范名称与定义表

规范名称	定　义
美国统一商业秘密法（Uniform Trade Secrets Act）	包含方程式、机制形态、编辑物、计算机程序、装置、方法、技术或程序等任何信息，这些信息：（1）在不被他人广泛知悉、不被他人轻易获得的情况下，具有事实上或潜在的独立经济价值；（2）而且这些信息必须尽合理的努力保持其秘密性。
美国经济间谍法案（EPA）	属于任何形式与种类的金融、商业、科学、技术、经济、或工程方面的信息；其中包括机制形态、计划书、出版物、程序设计、配方、设计图、模型、制造方法与技术、处理程序与制造过程、计算机程序、密码等。不论该信息是有形或无形、或其储存及收集的方式为何（电子、图案、照片或文字），只要符合：（1）其拥有者已尽合理的努力保持其秘密性；（2）不被公众广泛知悉或轻易获得的情况下，具有事实上或潜在的独立经济价值的，均可被视作为商业秘密。

续表

规范名称	定义
北美自由贸易区协议（NAFTA）	该信息：(1) 具有秘密性,并非经常接触该种类信息的人所共知或可轻易得知,不论该信息是一整体,或是有关具体的组成或是其零组件的组合等信息；(2) 必须要因其秘密性而有确实或是潜在的商业价值；(3) 合法控制该信息的人必须依其个别情况,已采取合理的步骤以保持其秘密性。各缔约成员国得要求,若欲取得商业秘密的保护,该商业秘密应通过文件、电磁方法、光盘、微缩片、影片或其他类似工具加以证明。

在与贸易相关的知识产权协议方面,只要符合下列三个条件,则不论自然人或法人,均应有防止他人未经其许可而以违背诚实商业行为的方法披露、获得或使用合法处于其控制下信息的可能：

(1) 在一定意义上属于秘密,即该信息作为整体或作为其中内容的确切组合,并非通常从事有关该信息工作领域的人所能普遍了解或容易获得的。

(2) 因其秘密性而具有商业价值。

(3) 合法控制该信息的人,为保护该秘密已经根据有关情况采取了合理措施。

从表 5-3 的定义中,可以了解商业秘密是以构成要件来进行判断,其要件在国际间大致相同,即必须具有秘密性、经济价值及合理的保密措施。另外,由表 5-3 立法例也可以看出,商业秘密的范围不限于科技类的信息,但是所列举的形态,如程序设计、配方、设计图、模型、制造方法与技术、处理程序与制造过程、计算机程序、密码等,都是属于科技成果的表现形式,显示"科技秘密"在商业秘密中占有重要分量。这种定义描述的方式,使用科技研发人员较熟悉的名词,也使其易于警觉到手边所接触的各种形态科技数据,都可能有保密需求；而一般保护商业秘密所采用的方法，包括研发单位必须建立合理保密措施、要求研发人员签署保密书等，也较"国家机密"、"秘密专利"等法制，更能针对科技研发的特性，达到"科技秘密"较周密的保密。

所以，对于政府要建立"国防科技秘密"的保密机制，本书认为应该要结合商业秘密的观念与法制，而不是一味立法介入研发活动，进行审查、管制、限制发表、征收研发成果财产权等干涉行为。例如，美国《经济间谍法案》就是利用商业秘密的观念，以政府提供刑事上的权力，保护民间企业所自行认定的商业秘密，对抗想以不正当方法取得美国民间研发成果的外国企业或政府，因此，相对于政府运用国家机密、限制科技信息发表、管制出口等制度，民间企业与研究机构的反对不会过于强烈，也同样能达到维护国家安全与经济利益的目的。因此，对于"国防科技秘密"的定义范围及保护方法而言，应该要同时考虑包含到"国家机密"及"商业秘密"两者，才能达到周延保密的目的。"国防科技秘密"的范围，不等同于"国家机密"或"商业秘密"，但是"国防科技秘密"应可区分为"国家机密"或"商业秘密"两种属性。例如，国防科技研发所完成的武器系统性能、规格、作用方式、核心技术、技术命令、操作手册等，可以经一定程序核定机密等级，按国家机密的制度保密；但其研发过程中，产生无数的研发成果数据，不可能完全纳入国家机密，例如，有些属于基础性或学术性的研究成果、测试数据，或是一般性机构运作的零件蓝图等，并无法窥出武器系统全貌，不致影响国家安全，也不应以国家机密制度要求保密，则此时应赋予研究单位一个权限，不论研发成果是归属政府或研究单位所有，都可以自行认定为商业秘密，仅能在合法及契约规范下作有限度的流通，兼顾国家保密及科技发展的需求。

当然，"国家机密"属于公共立法的规范领域，而"商业秘密"则属于企业或个人之间的保密措施，两者之间是否有冲突和交叉？

首先，从形式上看，两者间并不冲突，因为"国家机密"一般必须有明确的核定权责、程序、保密期限、标示等，所以在外观条件上应有明确辨识的基础，非属于国家机密的，才有进一步考虑以商业秘密保护的必要，不致有所抵触。其次，从实质上看，如果行政机关有事后作实质审认的权力，或必须由司法机关作最后审查确认，则确有可能产生问题，例如，被主管单位核定为"商业秘密"的资料，经事后审查认定为"国家机密"，那么那些属于善意的资料持有者，泄密行为的法律责任将有所争议。

事实上，各国对于"国家机密"的定义就存在采取实质定义或形式定义两种不同理论基础，采取实质概念定义的欧陆法，容许依据社会相当性的理论，具体按情况解释，或按正当业务的理由，主张其违法性的阻却；而采取形式定义的美国法，则以数据是否被分类指定，判断其得否公开的命运。

所以，本书认为，国防科技保密的法制，应该先形式上定义出"国防科技秘密"的名词，或其他类似名称，明确告知研发人员"国防科技秘密"中，属于"国家机密"受到法律规范的保密要求和负有刑事责任，对于不属于"国家机密"但仍有保密需求的，则以"商业秘密"方式保护，成果在使用上较有弹性，且对单位及研发人员的知识产权也有保障，让研发单位及人员乐于采取保密措施，达到政府希望的保密效果。当"国家机密"有明确的形式定义时，研发人员或信息持有者，看到数据上的标示都可以明确了解其保密法律责任；而当"国家机密"采取实质定义时，其与"商业秘密"之间可能会出现交叉，不论实质认定机密的界限怎样设定，其非机密的部分仍需辅以商业秘密保护，才能有效控制泄密的风险及损害。

至于对"国防科技秘密"的法律定义，依科技研发成果的特性及各国立法例，恐难以文字明确叙述或完整列举所有形态，大致上

第五章 国防科技保密机制建设争议与问题

可参考商业秘密法制，作概括加列举及构成要素的定义。针对国防科技保密制度是对民间研发活动的行政干涉，且国家机密又常有实质认定的问题，本书主张在"国防科技秘密"定义之外，仍必须对"国防科技秘密"的范围或项目，建立一个动态系统来审查界定，例如，组织一个公正客观的审查会议或专责单位，建立起属于"国家机密"或"敏感性"（需要其他适当保密或管制措施）的技术项目清单，用技术项目来涵盖该技术相关内容的信息，才能对国防科技保密的范围有所界定。而这样一个审查机制，必须与国家机密范围及科技出口管制项目清单，有整体性的设计或相互结合，而不是各自为政。

总而言之，本书主要的核心思想就是综合运用国家机密保护、国内科技保密、国际科技保密、商业秘密保护四种法律系统，建构国防科技保密法制规范。

第六章

启　示

　　本书以国防科技研发及技术转移过程中的保密需求，作为问题来源及研究主题，但在书中实际上已经全面探讨到与国家安全相关的整体性科学技术保密的法律制度。因为本书通过资料收集分析与研究论证发现，国防科技保密的规范是国家整体性科技保密法制的核心与基础；而国防科技保密制度的落实与效果的达成，无法靠单一法规或制定特别法来完成，还是必须从国家整体科技研究的成果管理与保密制度上全面研究落实。

　　这样的结论与现今国防科技研发环境改变及科学技术研发的特性，有重大关联性。就国防科技研发环境而言，现代战争已不是单纯军事武力的较量，而是一个国家整体政治、经济、科技等综合国力的竞争；毕竟传统上由国家自行投入资源进行国防武力建设的做法已不能满足需求，必须结合民间力量从事科技研发与产业整体发展，才能提高保障国家安全的力量。因此，科技研发成果信息在被鼓励公开交流以促进创新，及被要求适度保密以维护国家安全这两方面产生"拉锯"；所以，国防科技研发的保密必须是一种"免疫式"的管理保密系统，在无碍科技创新与技术转移的前提下，能达到维护国家安全的目的。也就是说，现代化国家已不能以政府体系内封闭式的系统满足国防科研目的，也无法以单独立法的手段，或

第六章 启　示

以特定的行政行为,就能解决科技保密问题。因此,从整体性的国家机密保护、国内科技保密、国际科技保密等法制,配合知识产权制度的运用,以检讨符合国防科技保密需求,并在执行面加以落实,才能最终满足国防科技保密目的。

再从科学技术研发的特性来看,为了应对科技的快速发展,管控无形知识流动所产生的风险,必须建立"动态式"的审查管理及保密系统。在无关国家安全的科技研究方面,同样有类似的管制需求,例如,基因科技对社会伦理产生的重大冲击;也必须应对科技的动态发展,和科技信息的不足或不易了解,建立弹性而动态的风险评价和审查机制,通过风险管控达到安全目的。

因此,就本书的观察研究结果看,国防科技保密的法制建立,应从上游关于政策制度目的、保密管制项目及审查原则先进行明确规定,才能进一步由相关主管机关制定配套措施,提供下游的科技研发单位及人员遵守之,为国家安全维护达到预防、免疫的功效。否则若仅以救火式的观念,针对个别泄密案件,头痛医头、脚痛医脚,反而可能对整体科学、社会发展造成危害,甚至有侵害公民基本权之虞。

就我国的情形看,针对国防科技保密的问题,国防技术转移法制与国家科技保护法制是处于同步推动中,更应该注重两者关联性,并加以整合;即政府推动国防科技转移民间的政策,应该先妥善制定国防科技保密制度,整理出属于国防核心能量的关键科技项目清单,作为基础及依据,才能进一步发展形成整体国家科技保护的管制范围。因此,本书建议参考美国军用关键技术清单(MCTL)的做法,订出国防科技(或影响国家安全)的关键科技项目作为基础,再邀集产官学研各界代表讨论,纳入影响我国科技实力及经济竞争力的敏感专门科学技术项目,以形成整体"国家科技保护"的管制范围,并建立审议检讨及对人民的补偿机制,使民间有明确的遵循依据。同时，对于现有法令中已有的相关制度，如《专利法》中的机密专利、《对外贸易法》中的高科技出口管制制度，也能配合整体"国家科技保护"需求，进行检讨修正及落实制度执行，才能完整建构国家科技保护机制、满足国防科技保密需求、达到维护国家安全及促进整体科技进步的双重目的！

参考文献

1. Alan S. Gutterman & Jacob N. Erlich, *Technology Development and Transfer : The Transactional and Legal Environment*, Quorum Books, 1997.
2. Alice P. Gast, *The Impact of Restricting Information Access on Science and Technology*. http://www.aau.edu/research/Gast.pdf (2004.2.24 visited).
3. Ari-Pekka Hameri, *Technology Transfer Between Basic Research and Industry*, Technovation, Vol.16, No.2, pp.51-57 (1995).
4. Arthur R. Miller & Michael H. Davis, *Intellectual Property: Patents, Trademarks, and Copyright*, West Publishing CO., 1983.
5. Assafa Endeshaw, *Commentary: A Critical Assessment of The U.S. - China Conflict on Intellectual Property*, 6 Alb. L.J. Sci. & Tech. (Albany Law Journal of Science & Technology), pp.295-338, 1996.
6. Dana A. Shea, *Balancing Scientific Publication and National Security Concerns: Issues for Congress*, Report for Congress, Order Code RL31695, January 10, 2003, http://www.aau.edu/research/science1.10.03.pdf.

7. Department of Defense Directive 5535.3, *DoD Domestic Technology Transfer Program*, May 21, 1999.

8. Department of Defense Instruction 5535.8, *DoD Domestic Technology Transfer Program Procedures*, May 14, 1999.

9. Genevieve J. Knezo, "*Sensitive But Unclassified*" *and Other Federal Security Controls on Scientific and Technical Information*: "*History and Current Controversy*", Report for Congress, Order Code RL31845, April 2 2003, http://www.fas.org/irp/crs/RL31845.pdf.

10. Gordon V. Smith & Russell L. Parr, *Intellectual Property: Licensing and Joint Venture Profit Strategies*, John Wiley & Sons, 1998.

11. Harvey Drucker, *Technology Transfer: A View from the Trenches*, http://www.piercelaw.edu/Risk/Vol5/spring/Drucjer.htm (2003.8.5 visited).

12. Henry Cohen, *Freedom of Speech and Press: Exceptions to the First Amendment*, CRS Report for Congress, Order Code 95-815A, Updates August 27, 2003, http://www.fas.org/irp/crs/95-815.pdf.

13. Ian F. Fergusson, *The Expotr Administration Act: Evolution, Provisions, and Debate*, Report for Congress, Order Code RL31832, April 1, 2004, http://www.aau.edu/research/RL31832.pdf.

14. James P. Chandler, *The Loss of New Technology to Foreign Competitors: U.S. Companies Must Search for Protective Solutions*, 27 GW J. Int'l L. & Econ. (George Washington Journal of International Law & Economics), pp.305-325, 1993-1994.

15. Jeff Dale & David Furneaux, *The State Role in Effective Technology Transfer*, http://www.ncsl.org/programs/esnr/96tech.htm (2003.8.5 visited).

16. John A. Alic, Lewis M. Branscomb, Harvey Brooks, Ashton B.

Carter, Gerald L. Epstein, *Beyond Spinoff*, Harvard Business School Press, 1992.

17. John D. Podesta, *Shadow Creep: Government Secrecy Since 9/11*, University of Illinois Journal of Law, Technology and Policy, Fall 2002, pp. 361 – 372.

18. John E. Mauk, Note: *The Slippery Slope of Secrecy: Why Patent Law Preempts Reverse – Engineering Clauses in Shrink – Wrap Licenses*, 43 Wm and Mary L. Rev. (William & Mary Law Review), pp.819 – 849, December, 2001.

19. Judith Reppy, ed., *Secrecy and Knowledge Production*. Cornell University Peace Studies Program Occasional Paper #23, October 1999, http://www.einaudi.cornell.edu/PeaceProgram /publications/occasional _papers/occasi onal – paper23.pdf.

20. Lawrence Rudolph, *Overview of Federal Technology Transfer*, http://www.piercelaw.edu/Risk/Vol5/spring/Rudolph.htm (2003.8.5 visited).

21. Matthew Crane, *U.S. Export Controls on Technology Transfer*, Duke Law & Technology Review, August 29 2001, pp. 1 – 10.

22. National Academy of Science, *A Question of Balance : Private Rights and the Public Interest in Scientific and Technical Database*, National Academy Press, Washington, D.C., 1999.

23. *National Industrial Security Program Operational Manual* (1995 NISPOM incorporating Change One (July 1997) & Change Two (Feb 2001)), http://www.dss.mil/isec/nispom.htm 2003.10.27.

24. Robert C. Haldiman, *Intellectual Property : Policy Considerations From A Practitioner's Perspective : Prior User Rights for Business Method Patents*, 20 St. Louis U. Pub. L. Rev. (Saint Louis University Public Law

Review), pp. 245-280, 2001.

25. Robert P. Benko, *Protecting Intellectual Property Rights: Issues and Controversies*, American Enterprise Institute for Public Policy Research, Washington, D.C., 1987.

26. Rogert P. Merges, Peter S. Menell & Mark A. Lenley, *Intellectual Property in the New Technological Age*, Aspen Law & Business, 2000.

27. Sabing H. Lee, *Protecting The Private Inventor Under The Peacetime: Provisions of The Invention Secrecy Act*, http://www.law.berkeley.edu/journals/btlj/articles/ vol12/Lee/html/ text.html (2003.9.14 visited).

28. Steven Aftergood, *Secrecy Is Back in Fashion*, Bulletin of the Atomic Scientists, Vol.56 Issue 6, pp.24-31, Nov/Dec, 2000.

29. Steven B, Winters, John A. Bolmgren, *How The US Government Controls Technology*, Computer and Internet Lawyer, January 2002, pp.1-5.

30. Yu. A. Bobylov, *Security Classification in Fundamental Science*, Military Thought, Vol.9, Issue 1, p.67-76 (January 2000).

附录 1
法案、专有名词中英文对照表

中文译名	英文原文	英文缩写
军民两用技术	dual use technology	DUT
拜杜法案	Bayh–Dole Act, 1980	
怀德技术创新法案	The Stevenson–Wydler Technology Innovation Act, 1980	
联邦技术转移法	Federal Technology Transfer Act, 1986	
国防科技转换、转投资及转移协助法案	Defense Technology Conversion, Reinvestment, Transition and Assistance Act	DTCRTAA
能源部		DOE
商务部		DOC
国家标准技术院		NIST
国家科学基金会		NSD
国家航空太空总署		NASA
国防部先进研究计划局		DARPA
技术转投资项目计划	Technology Reinvestment Program,	TRP

续表

中文译名	英文原文	英文缩写
德国"联邦安全检查法"第四条,即对政府的"秘密事项"	Verschluβ sahen	
多边出口管制协调委员会	Coordinating Committee for Multilateral Export Control	COCOM
瓦圣那协议	The Wassenaar Arrangement	WA
导弹技术管制协议		MTCR
核武器国集团		NSG
澳洲集团		AG
联合国禁止化学武器公约执行机构 OPCW	the Organization for the Prohibition of Chemical Weapons	
第189号国家安全决定指令	National Security Decision Directive 189,	NSDD 189
敏感性但非属机密信息	sensitive but unclassified,	SBU
第145号国家安全决定指令	National Security Decision Directive 145	NSDD-145
联邦政府电子通讯及自动化信息系统中敏感性但非属机密信息的保护政策	National Policy on Protection of Sensitive, but unclassified Information in Federal Government Telecommunications and Automated Information Systems	NTISSP No.2
美国爱国者法案	USA Patriot Act of 2001	USA PA
国土安全法案	Homeland Security Act of 2002	
保护与国土安全有关的大规模破坏武器和其他敏感文件信息的行动	Action to Safeguard Information Regarding Weapons of Mass Destruction and Other Sensitive Documents Related to Homeland Security	
国家档案总署	National Archives and Records Administration	
信息安全监督办公室	Information Security Oversight Office	ISOO
国土安全办公室	Office of Homeland Security	

附录1 法案、专有名词中英文对照表

续表

中文译名	英文原文	英文缩写
与美国国土安全有关的敏感性信息	sensitive information related to America's homeland security	SHSI
信息自由法案		FOIA
发明秘密法案	Invention Secrecy Act	
陆海军专利顾问委员会	Army and Navy Patent Advisory Board	ANPAB
军事服务专利顾问委员会	Armed Services Patent Advisory Board	ASPAB
发明秘密法案	Invention Secrecy Act of 1951	
信息自由法案		FOIA
联合国禁止化学武器公约		CWC
出口管理法	Export Administration Act	
出口管理规则	Export Administration Regulations	EAR
武器出口管制法	Arms Export Control Act	
国际间武器管制规则	International Traffic in Arms Regulations	ITAR
卫星或太空载具的整合发射系统或导弹技术管制条约	Missile Technology Control Regime	MTCR
侵权行为法汇编	Restatement of Torts,§757	
统一州法全国委员会	National Conference of Commissioners on Uniform State Laws	
经济间谍法案	The Economic Espionage Act	EEA
习惯法	Common Law	
指令	Directive	
指示	Instruction	
国防部信息安全计划	DOD Information Security Program,DOD 5200.1-R	
仅为官方使用	For Official Use Only	FOUO
国家产业安全计划		NISP

续表

中文译名	英文原文	英文缩写
国家安全委员会	National Security Council	
信息安全监督局	Information Security Oversight Office	ISOO
国家产业安全计划作业手册	National Industrial Security Program, Operational Manual	NISPOM
审认安全机构	Cognizant Security Agency	CSA
国防部对研究及技术保护的规定程序	Mandatory Procedures for Research and Technology Protection Within the DOD	
审认安全办公室	Cognizant Security Offices	CSO
国防授权法案	National Defense Authorization Act for Fiscal Year 1993	
技术转移办公室	Office of Technology Transition	
国家安全机密	Genuine national security secrecy	
政治上的秘密	Political secrecy	
官僚式的秘密	Bureaucratic secrecy	
美国爱国者法案	USA Patriot Act of 2001	
国土安全法案	Homeland Security Act of 2002	
联合安全委员会	Joint Security Commission	
中央情报局		CIA
美国科学家协会	Federation of American Scientists	FAS
隐私法	Privacy Act of 1974, 5USC 552a	
计算机安全法案	Computer Security Act of 1987, relevant portions codified at 15 USC 278 g-3	
会审总局	General Accounting Office	GAO
卡德备忘录	Card Memo	

附录1　法案、专有名词中英文对照表

续表

中文译名	英文原文	英文缩写
跨部门安全机密等级审议会	Interagency Security Classification Appeals Panel	
平衡原则	balancing test	
司法审查	judicial review	
武装服务专利委员会	Armed Services Patent Advisory Board	ASPAB
原子能法	Atomic Energy Act of 1954	
国家学术学会	National Academies	
公开前审查	Pre–Publication Review	
美国军民两用货品出口管制是由商务部的产业安全局	Bureau of Industry and Security	BIS
国防贸易管制办公室	Office of Defense Trade Controls	ODTC
联邦调查局		FBI
美国工业安全协会	American Society for Industrial Security	ASIS
1996经济间谍法案	The Economic Espionage Act of 1996	
州际传输盗用财产法	Interstate Transportation of Stolen Property Act, 18 U.S.C. Sec. 2314	
邮件诈欺	mail fraud	
通讯诈欺	wire fraud	
超越合理怀疑	Beyond Reasonable Doubt	
曼哈顿计划	Manhattan Project	
权力行政又称权威行政	hoheitliche Verwaltung	
干涉行政或译为侵害行政	Eingriffsverwaltung	
介入权	march–in right	
合理补偿	just compensation	
国有	government–owned	
政府控制	government–controlled	

续表

中文译名	英文原文	英文缩写
财产上的利益	property interest	
维吉尼亚权利法案	Bill of Rights Virginia	
追求真理说	truth – seeking theory	
言论自由市场说	theory of marketplace of ideas	
健全民主程序说	democratic；process theory；	
表现自由说	self – expression theory	
实现自我说	self – fulfillment or self – realization theory	
通讯法案	Communications Act of 1934	
美国联邦通讯委员会	Federal Communication Commission	
五角大楼文件案	the Pentagon Paper	
明显而立即危险	clear and present danger test	
知情权	right to know	
猥亵	obscenity	
儿童色情	child pornography	
电子信息自由法	Electronic Freedom of Information Act	E – FOIA
军事关键技术清单	Militarily Critical Technologies List	MCTL
出口管理规则	Export Administration Regulations，EAR	
与国防物品直接有关的	International Traffic in Arms Regulations	ITAR
国家产业安全计划作业手册	National Industrial Security Program Operating ITAR（22 CFR 120.1 – 130.17，1987）	
美国统一商业秘密法	Uniform Trade Secrets Act	
美国经济间谍法案		EPA
北美自由贸易区协议		NAFTA

附录 2
美国《拜杜法案》[①]（Bayh – Dole Act, 1980）

– CITE –

35 USC CHAPTER 18 – PATENT RIGHTS IN INVENTIONS MADE WITH FEDERAL ASSISTANCE

01/03/05

– EXPCITE –

TITLE 35 – PATENTS

PART II – PATENTABILITY OF INVENTIONS AND GRANT OF PATENTS

CHAPTER 18 – PATENT RIGHTS IN INVENTIONS MADE WITH FEDERAL ASSISTANCE

– HEAD –

CHAPTER 18 – PATENT RIGHTS IN INVENTIONS MADE WITH

[①] 法案文字引自美国政府网站，条文仅供参考，本书不对文字准确性负责。

FEDERAL ASSISTANCE

– MISC1 –

Sec.

200.	Policy and objective.
201.	Definitions.
202.	Disposition of rights.
203.	March – in rights.
204.	Preference for United States industry.
205.	Confidentiality.
206.	Uniform clauses and regulations.
207.	Domestic and foreign protection of federally owned inventions.
208.	Regulations governing Federal licensing.
209.	Licensing federally owned inventions.
210.	Precedence of chapter.
211.	Relationship to antitrust laws.
212.	Disposition of rights in educational awards.

AMENDMENTS

2000 – Pub. L. 106 – 404, Sec. 4(b), Nov. 1, 2000, 114 Stat. 1744, substituted "Licensing federally owned inventions" for "Restrictions on licensing of federally owned inventions" in item 209.

1984 – Pub. L. 98 – 620, title V, Sec. 501(15), Nov. 8, 1984, 98 Stat. 3368, added item 212.

1982 – Pub. L. 97 – 256, title I, Sec. 101(5), Sept. 8, 1982, 96 Stat. 816, redesignated chapter 38, as added by Pub. L. 96 – 517, Sec. 6(a), Dec. 12, 1980, 94 Stat. 3018, comprising sections 200

附录 2 美国《拜杜法案》(Bayh – Dole Act, 1980)

to 211, as chapter 18, and transferred chapter 18, as so redesignated, to end of this part from end of part IV.

– End –

– CITE –

35 USC Sec. 200   01/03/05

– EXPCITE –

TITLE 35 – PATENTS

PART II – PATENTABILITY OF INVENTIONS AND GRANT OF PATENTS

CHAPTER 18 – PATENT RIGHTS IN INVENTIONS MADE WITH FEDERAL ASSISTANCE

– HEAD –

Sec. 200. Policy and objective

– STATUTE –

It is the policy and objective of the Congress to use the patent system to promote the utilization of inventions arising from federally supported research or development; to encourage maximum participation of small business firms in federally supported research and development efforts; to promote collaboration between commercial concerns and nonprofit organizations, including universities; to ensure that inventions made by nonprofit organizations and small business firms are used in a manner to promote free competition and enterprise without unduly encumbering future research and discovery; to promote the commercialization and public availability of inventions made in the United States by United States industry and labor; to ensure that the Government obtains sufficient rights in federally supported inventions to meet the needs of the Government and protect the public against nonuse or unreasonable use of inventions; and to minimize the costs of administering policies in this area.

– SOURCE –

(Added Pub. L. 96 – 517, Sec. 6(a), Dec. 12, 1980, 94 Stat. 3018;

amended Pub. L. 106 – 404, Sec. 5, Nov. 1, 2000, 114 Stat. 1745.)

– MISC1 –

AMENDMENTS

2000 – Pub. L. 106 – 404 substituted "enterprise without unduly encumbering future research and discovery;" for "enterprise;".

EFFECTIVE DATE

Chapter effective July 1, 1981, but implementing regulations authorized to be issued earlier, see section 8(f) of Pub. L. 96 – 517, set out as an Effective Date of 1980 Amendment note under section 41 of this title.

附录2 美国《拜杜法案》(Bayh – Dole Act, 1980)

- End -

- CITE -
  35 USC Sec. 201   01/03/05

- EXPCITE -
  TITLE 35 – PATENTS
  PART II – PATENTABILITY OF INVENTIONS AND GRANT OF PATENTS
  CHAPTER 18 – PATENT RIGHTS IN INVENTIONS MADE WITH FEDERAL ASSISTANCE

- HEAD -
  Sec. 201. Definitions

- STATUTE -

As used in this chapter –

(a) The term "Federal agency" means any executive agency as defined in section 105 of title 5, and the military departments as defined by section 102 of title 5.

(b) The term "funding agreement" means any contract, grant, or cooperative agreement entered into between any Federal agency, other than the Tennessee Valley Authority, and any contractor for the performance of experimental, developmental, or research work funded in whole or in part by the Federal Government. Such term includes any assignment, substitution of parties, or subcontract of any type entered into for the performance of experimental, developmental, or research work under a funding agreement as herein defined.

(c) The term "contractor" means any person, small business firm, or nonprofit organization that is a party to a funding agreement.

(d) The term "invention" means any invention or discovery which is or may be patentable or otherwise protectable under this title or any novel variety of plant which is or may be protectable under the Plant Variety Protection Act (7 U.S.C. 2321 et seq.).

(e) The term "subject invention" means any invention of the contractor conceived or first actually reduced to practice in the performance of work under a funding agreement: Provided, That in the case of a variety of plant, the date of determination (as defined in section 41(d)(!1) of the Plant Variety Protection Act (7 U.S.C. 2401(d))) must also occur during the period of contract performance.

(f) The term "practical application" means to manufacture in the case of a composition or product, to practice in the case of a process or method, or to operate in the case of a machine or system; and, in each case, under such conditions as to establish that the invention is being utilized and that its benefits are to the extent permitted by law or Government regulations available to the public on reasonable terms.

(g) The term "made" when used in relation to any invention means the conception or first actual reduction to practice of such invention.

(h) The term "small business firm" means a small business concern as defined at section 2 of Public Law 85 – 536 (15 U.S.C. 632) and implementing regulations of the Administrator of the Small Business Administration. (i) The term "nonprofit organization" means universities

附录2 美国《拜杜法案》（Bayh – Dole Act, 1980)

and other institutions of higher education or an organization of the type described in section 501(c)(3) of the Internal Revenue Code of 1986 (26 U.S.C. 501(c)) and exempt from taxation under section 501(a) of the Internal Revenue Code (26 U.S.C. 501(a)) or any nonprofit scientific or educational organization qualified under a State nonprofit organization statute.

– SOURCE –

(Added Pub. L. 96 – 517, Sec. 6(a), Dec. 12, 1980, 94 Stat. 3019;

amended Pub. L. 98 – 620, title V, Sec. 501(1), (2), Nov. 8, 1984, 98 Stat. 3364; Pub. L. 99 – 514, Sec. 2, Oct. 22, 1986, 100 Stat. 2095;

Pub. L. 107 – 273, div. C, title III, Sec. 13206(a)(12), Nov. 2, 2002, 116 Stat. 1904.)

– REFTEXT –

REFERENCES IN TEXT

The Plant Variety Protection Act, referred to in subsec. (d), is Pub. L. 91 – 577, Dec. 24, 1970, 84 Stat. 1542, as amended, which is classified principally to chapter 57 (Sec. 2321 et seq.) of Title 7, Agriculture. For complete classification of this Act to the Code, see Short Title note set out under section 2321 of Title 7 and Tables.

Section 41 of the Plant Variety Protection Act (7 U.S.C. 2401 (d)), referred to in subsec. (e), was subsequently amended, and no longer defines the term "date of determination".

- MISC1 -

AMENDMENTS

2002 - Subsec. (a). Pub. L. 107-273 struck out "United States Code," after "section 105 of title 5," and, "United States Code" after "section 102 of title 5".

1986 - Subsec. (i). Pub. L. 99-514 substituted "Internal Revenue Code of 1986" for "Internal Revenue Code of 1954".

1984 - Subsec. (d). Pub. L. 98-620, Sec. 501(1), inserted "or any novel variety of plant which is or may be protectable under the Plant Variety Protection Act (7 U.S.C. 2321 et seq.)" after "title".

Subsec. (e). Pub. L. 98-620, Sec. 501(2), inserted: "Provided, That in the case of a variety of plant, the date of determination (as defined in section 41(d) of the Plant Variety Protection Act (7 U.S.C. 2401(d))) must also occur during the period of contract performance" after "agreement".

- FOOTNOTE -

(!1) See References in Text note below.

- End -

- CITE -

35 USC Sec. 202   01/03/05

- EXPCITE -

TITLE 35 - PATENTS

附录 2　美国《拜杜法案》(Bayh – Dole Act, 1980)

PART II – PATENTABILITY OF INVENTIONS AND GRANT OF PATENTS

CHAPTER 18 – PATENT RIGHTS IN INVENTIONS MADE WITH FEDERAL ASSISTANCE

– HEAD –

Sec. 202. Disposition of rights

– STATUTE –

(a) Each nonprofit organization or small business firm may, within a reasonable time after disclosure as required by paragraph (c)(1) of this section, elect to retain title to any subject invention: Provided, however, That a funding agreement may provide otherwise (i) when the contractor is not located in the United States or does not have a place of business located in the United States or is subject to the control of a foreign government, (ii) in exceptional circumstances when it is determined by the agency that restriction or elimination of the right to retain title to any subject invention will better promote the policy and objectives of this chapter (iii) when it is determined by a Government authority which is authorized by statute or Executive order to conduct foreign intelligence or counter – intelligence activities that the restriction or elimination of the right to retain title to any subject invention is necessary to protect the security of such activities or, (iv) when the funding agreement includes the operation of a Government – owned, contractor – operated facility of the Department of Energy primarily dedicated to that Department's naval nuclear propulsion or weapons related programs and all funding agreement limitations under this subparagraph on the contractor's right to elect title to a subject invention are limited to inventions occurring under the above two programs of the Department of Energy. The rights of the nonprofit organization or small business firm shall be subject to the provisions of paragraph (c) of this section and the other provisions of this chapter.

(b)(1) The rights of the Government under subsection (a) shall not be exercised by a Federal agency unless it first determines that at least one of the conditions identified in clauses (i) through (iv) of subsection (a) exists. Except in the case of subsection (a)(iii), the agency shall file with the Secretary of Commerce, within thirty days after the award of the applicable funding agreement, a copy of such determination. In the case of a determination under subsection (a)(ii), the statement shall include an analysis justifying the determination. In the case of determinations applicable to funding agreements with small business firms, copies shall also be sent to the Chief Counsel for Advocacy of the Small Business Administration. If the Secretary of Commerce believes that any individual determination or pattern of determinations is contrary to the policies and objectives of this chapter or otherwise not in conformance with this chapter, the Secretary shall so advise the head of the agency concerned and the Administrator of the Office of Federal Procurement Policy, and recommend corrective actions.

(2) Whenever the Administrator of the Office of Federal Procurement Policy has determined that one or more Federal agencies are utilizing the authority of clause (i) or (ii) of subsection (a) of this section in a manner that is contrary to the policies and objectives of this chapter, the Administrator is authorized to issue regulations describing classes of

附录2 美国《拜杜法案》(Bayh – Dole Act, 1980)

situations in which agencies may not exercise the authorities of those clauses.

(3) At least once every 5 years, the Comptroller General shall transmit a report to the Committees on the Judiciary of the Senate and House of Representatives on the manner in which this chapter is being implemented by the agencies and on such other aspects of Government patent policies and practices with respect to federally funded inventions as the Comptroller General believes appropriate.

(4) If the contractor believes that a determination is contrary to the policies and objectives of this chapter or constitutes an abuse of discretion by the agency, the determination shall be subject to the (!1)section 203(b).

(c) Each funding agreement with a small business firm or nonprofit organization shall contain appropriate provisions to effectuate the following:

(1) That the contractor disclose each subject invention to the Federal agency within a reasonable time after it becomes known to contractor personnel responsible for the administration of patent matters, and that the Federal Government may receive title to any subject invention not disclosed to it within such time.

(2) That the contractor make a written election within two years after disclosure to the Federal agency (or such additional time as may be approved by the Federal agency) whether the contractor will retain title to a subject invention: Provided, That in any case where publication, on sale, or public use, has initiated the one year statutory period in which valid patent protection can still be obtained in the United States,

the period for election may be shortened by the Federal agency to a date that is not more than sixty days prior to the end of the statutory period: And provided further, That the Federal Government may receive title to any subject invention in which the contractor does not elect to retain rights or fails to elect rights within such times.

(3) That a contractor electing rights in a subject invention agrees to file a patent application prior to any statutory bar date that may occur under this title due to publication, on sale, or public use, and shall thereafter file corresponding patent applications in other countries in which it wishes to retain title within reasonable times, and that the Federal Government may receive title to any subject inventions in the United States or other countries in which the contractor has not filed patent applications on the subject invention within such times.

(4) With respect to any invention in which the contractor elects rights, the Federal agency shall have a nonexclusive, nontransferrable, irrevocable, paid-up license to practice or have practiced for or on behalf of the United States any subject invention throughout the world: Provided, That the funding agreement may provide for such additional rights, including the right to assign or have assigned foreign patent rights in the subject invention, as are determined by the agency as necessary for meeting the obligations of the United States under any treaty, international agreement, arrangement of cooperation, memorandum of understanding, or similar arrangement, including military agreement relating to weapons development and production.

(5) The right of the Federal agency to require periodic reporting on the utilization or efforts at obtaining utilization that are being made by the contractor or his licensees or assignees: Provided, That any such

附录2　美国《拜杜法案》（Bayh – Dole Act, 1980）

information as well as any information on utilization or efforts at obtaining utilization obtained as part of a proceeding under section 203 of this chapter shall be treated by the Federal agency as commercial and financial information obtained from a person and privileged and confidential and not subject to disclosure under section 552 of title 5.

(6) An obligation on the part of the contractor, in the event a United States patent application is filed by or on its behalf or by any assignee of the contractor, to include within the specification of such application and any patent issuing thereon, a statement specifying that the invention was made with Government support and that the Government has certain rights in the invention.

(7) In the case of a nonprofit organization, (A) a prohibition upon the assignment of rights to a subject invention in the United States without the approval of the Federal agency, except where such assignment is made to an organization which has as one of its primary functions the management of inventions (provided that such assignee shall be subject to the same provisions as the contractor); (B) a requirement that the contractor share royalties with the inventor; (C) except with respect to a funding agreement for the operation of a Government – owned – contractor – operated facility, a requirement that the balance of any royalties or income earned by the contractor with respect to subject inventions, after payment of expenses (including payments to inventors) incidental to the administration of subject inventions, be utilized for the support of scientific research or education; (D) a requirement that, except where it proves infeasible after a reasonable inquiry, in the licensing of subject inventions shall be given to small business firms; and (E) with respect to a funding

agreement for the operation of a Government – owned – contractor – operated facility, requirements (i) that after payment of patenting costs, licensing costs, payments to inventors, and other expenses incidental to the administration of subject inventions, 100 percent of the balance of any royalties or income earned and retained by the contractor during any fiscal year up to an amount equal to 5 percent of the annual budget of the facility, shall be used by the contractor for scientific research, development, and education consistent with the research and development mission and objectives of the facility, including activities that increase the licensing potential of other inventions of the facility; provided that if said balance exceeds 5 percent of the annual budget of the facility, that 75 percent of such excess shall be paid to the Treasury of the United States and the remaining 25 percent shall be used for the same purposes as described above in this clause (D); and (ii) that, to the extent it provides the most effective technology transfer, the licensing of subject inventions shall be administered by contractor employees on location at the facility.

(8) The requirements of sections 203 and 204 of this chapter.

(d) If a contractor does not elect to retain title to a subject invention in cases subject to this section, the Federal agency may consider and after consultation with the contractor grant requests for retention of rights by the inventor subject to the provisions of this Act and regulations promulgated hereunder.

(e) In any case when a Federal employee is a coinventor of any

附录2 美国《拜杜法案》(Bayh – Dole Act, 1980)

invention made with a nonprofit organization, a small business firm, or a non – Federal inventor, the Federal agency employing such coinventor may, for the purpose of consolidating rights in the invention and if it finds that it would expedite the development of the invention –

(1) license or assign whatever rights it may acquire in the subject invention to the nonprofit organization, small business firm, or non – Federal inventor in accordance with the provisions of this chapter; or

(2) acquire any rights in the subject invention from the nonprofit organization, small business firm, or non – Federal inventor, but only to the extent the party from whom the rights are acquired voluntarily enters into the transaction and no other transaction under this chapter is conditioned on such acquisition.

(f)(1) No funding agreement with a small business firm or nonprofit organization shall contain a provision allowing a Federal agency to require the licensing to third parties of inventions owned by the contractor that are not subject inventions unless such provision has been approved by the head of the agency and a written justification has been signed by the head of the agency. Any such provision shall clearly state whether the licensing may be required in connection with the practice of a subject invention, a specifically identified work object, or both. The head of the agency may not delegate the authority to approve provisions or sign justifications required by this paragraph.

(2) A Federal agency shall not require the licensing of third parties under any such provision unless the head of the agency determines that the use of the invention by others is necessary for the practice of a subject invention or for the use of a work object of the funding

agreement and that such action is necessary to achieve the practical application of the subject invention or work object. Any such determination shall be on the record after an opportunity for an agency hearing. Any action commenced for judicial review of such determination shall be brought within sixty days after notification of such determination.

– SOURCE –

(Added Pub. L. 96 – 517, Sec. 6(a), Dec. 12, 1980, 94 Stat. 3020; amended Pub. L. 98 – 620, title V, Sec. 501(3) – (8), Nov. 8, 1984, 98 Stat. 3364 – 3366; Pub. L. 102 – 204, Sec. 10, Dec. 10, 1991, 105 Stat. 1641; Pub. L. 106 – 113, div. B, Sec. 1000 (a)(9)[title IV, Sec.4732(a)(12)], Nov. 29, 1999, 113 Stat. 1536, 1501A – 583; Pub. L. 106 – 404, Sec. 6(1), Nov. 1, 2000, 114 Stat. 1745; Pub. L. 107 – 273, div. C, title III, Sec. 13206(a)(13), Nov. 2, 2002, 116 Stat. 1905.)

– REFTEXT –
REFERENCES IN TEXT

This Act, referred to in subsec.(d), probably means Pub. L. 96 – 517, Dec. 12, 1980, 94 Stat. 3015, which enacted sections 200 to 211 and 301 to 307 of this title, amended sections 41, 42, and 154 of this title, section 1113 of Title 15, Commerce and Trade, sections 101 and 117 of Title 17, Copyrights, and sections 2186, 2457, and 5908 of Title 42, The Public Health and Welfare, and enacted provisions set out as notes under sections 13 and 41 of this title. For complete classification of this Act to the Code, see Tables.

附录 2 美国《拜杜法案》(Bayh – Dole Act, 1980)

– MISC1 –

AMENDMENTS

2002 – Subsec. (b)(4). Pub. L. 107 – 273, Sec. 13206(a) (13)(A), substituted "section 203(b)" for "last paragraph of section 203(2)".

Subsec. (c)(4). Pub. L. 107 – 273, Sec. 13206(a)(13)(B) (i), substituted "additional rights," for "additional rights;".

Subsec. (c)(5). Pub. L. 107 – 273, Sec. 13206(a)(13)(B) (ii), struck out "of the United States Code" after "section 552 of title 5".

2000 – Subsec. (e). Pub. L. 106 – 404 amended subsec. (e) generally. Prior to amendment, subsec. (e) read as follows: "In any case when a Federal employee is a coinventor of any invention made under a funding agreement with a nonprofit organization or small business firm, the Federal agency employing such coinventor is authorized to transfer or assign whatever rights it may acquire in the subject invention from its employee to the contractor subject to the conditions set forth in this chapter."

1999 – Subsec. (a). Pub. L. 106 – 113, in first sentence, substituted "(iv)" for "(iv)" and struck out a second period at end.

1991 – Subsec. (b)(3). Pub. L. 102 – 204 substituted "every 5 years" for "each year".

1984 – Subsec. (a). Pub. L. 98 – 620, Sec. 501(3), substituted "when the contractor is not located in the United States or does not have a place of business located in the United States or is subject to the control of a foreign government" for "when the funding agreement is for the operation of a Government-owned research or production facility", struck out "or" before "(ii)", which was executed by striking out "or" before "(iii)" as the probable intent of Congress, and added cl. (iv).

Subsec. (b)(1). Pub. L. 98-620, Sec. 501(4), gave to the Department of Commerce oversight of agency use of the exceptions to small business or nonprofit organization invention ownership.

Subsec. (b)(2). Pub. L. 98-620, Sec. 501(4), substituted provisions authorizing the Administrator of the Office of Federal Procurement Policy to issue regulations describing situations in which agencies may not exercise the authorities of clauses (i) or (ii) of subsec. (a), whenever the Administrator has determined that one or more agencies are utilizing such authority in violation of this chapter for provisions which gave to the Comptroller General oversight of agency actions under this chapter.

Subsec. (b)(4). Pub. L. 98-620, Sec. 501(4A), added par. (4).

Subsec. (c)(1). Pub. L. 98-620, Sec. 501(5), substituted provisions requiring disclosure of each invention within a reasonable time after it becomes known to contractor personnel responsible for the administration of patent matters for provision requiring disclosure of each invention within a reasonable time after it is made.

Subsec. (c)(2). Pub. L. 98-620, Sec. 501(5), substituted provisions requiring the contractor to make a written election within two years after disclosure to the Federal agency (or such additional time as may be approved by the Federal agency) whether the contractor will retain title to a subject invention for provision requiring election to retain title within a reasonable time after disclosure, and inserted

附录 2 美国《拜杜法案》(Bayh – Dole Act, 1980)

provision authorizing the Federal agency to shorten the period for election under certain circumstances.

Subsec. (c)(3). Pub. L. 98 – 620, Sec. 501(5), substituted provisions requiring a contractor electing rights in a subject invention to file a patent application prior to any statutory bar date that may occur under this title due to publication, on sale, or public use, and thereafter to file corresponding patent applications in other countries in which it wishes to retain title within reasonable times for provisions requiring the contractor to file patent applications within a reasonable time.

Subsec. (c)(4). Pub. L. 98 – 620, Sec. 501(5), substituted provision that the funding agreement may provide for such additional rights, including the right to assign or have assigned foreign patent rights in the subject invention, as are determined by the agency as necessary for meeting the obligations of the United States under any treaty, international agreement, arrangement of cooperation, memorandum of understanding, or similar arrangement, including any military agreement relating to weapons development and production for provision that the agency could, if provided in the funding agreement, have additional rights to sublicense any foreign government or international organization pursuant to any existing or future treaty or agreement.

Subsec. (c)(5). Pub. L. 98 – 620, Sec. 501(6), substituted "as well as any information on utilization or efforts at obtaining utilization obtained as part of a proceeding under section 203 of this chapter shall be treated" for "may be treated".

Subsec. (c)(7)(A). Pub. L. 98 – 620, Sec. 501(7), struck out provision which made an exception for organizations which were not themselves engaged in or did not hold a substantial interest in other organizations engaged in the manufacture or sales of products or the use of processes that might utilize the invention or be in competition with embodiments of the invention.

Subsec. (c)(7)(B). Pub. L. 98 – 620, Sec. 501(8), redesignated cl. (C) as (B). Former cl. (B), relating to a prohibition against the granting of exclusive licenses under United States Patents or Patent Applications in a subject invention by the contractor to persons other than small business firms for periods in excess of certain specified periods and relating to commercial sales, was struck out.

Subsec.(c)(7)(C). Pub.L.98 – 620, Sec.501(8), added cl.(C). Former cl. (C) redesignated (B).

Subsec. (c)(7)(D). Pub. L. 98 – 620, Sec. 501(8), added cl. (D). Former cl. (D) redesignated (E).

Subsec.(c)(7)(E). Pub.L.98 – 620, Sec.501(8), redesignated former cl. (D) as (E) and inserted provisions placing a limit on the amount of royalties that the contract operators of Government – owned laboratories are entitled to retain after paying patent administrative expenses and a share of the royalties to inventors, requiring payment of amounts in excess of such limits to the United States Treasury, and requiring that, to the extent it provides the most effective technology transfer, the licensing of subject inventions shall be administered by contractor employees on location at the facility.

附录2 美国《拜杜法案》(Bayh – Dole Act, 1980)

EFFECTIVE DATE OF 1999 AMENDMENT

Amendment by Pub. L. 106 – 113 effective 4 months after Nov. 29, 1999, see section 1000(a)(9)[title IV, Sec. 4731] of Pub. L. 106 – 113, set out as a note under section 1 of this title.

– FOOTNOTE –

(!1)So in original. The word "the" probably should not appear.

– End –

– CITE –

35 USC Sec. 203　　　　　　　　　　　　　　　　　01/03/05

– EXPCITE –

TITLE 35 – PATENTS

PART II – PATENTABILITY OF INVENTIONS AND GRANT OF PATENTS

CHAPTER 18 – PATENT RIGHTS IN INVENTIONS MADE WITH FEDERAL ASSISTANCE

– HEAD –

Sec. 203. March – in rights

– STATUTE –

(a) With respect to any subject invention in which a small business firm or nonprofit organization has acquired title under this chapter, the Federal agency under whose funding agreement the subject invention was made shall have the right, in accordance with such procedures as are provided in regulations promulgated hereunder to require the contractor, an assignee or exclusive licensee of a subject invention to grant a nonexclusive, partially exclusive, or exclusive license in any field of use to a responsible applicant or applicants, upon terms that are reasonable under the circumstances, and if the contractor, assignee, or exclusive licensee refuses such request, to grant such a license itself, if the Federal agency determines that such —

(1) action is necessary because the contractor or assignee has not taken, or is not expected to take within a reasonable time, effective steps to achieve practical application of the subject invention in such field of use;

(2) action is necessary to alleviate health or safety needs which are not reasonably satisfied by the contractor, assignee, or their licensees;

(3) action is necessary to meet requirements for public use specified by Federal regulations and such requirements are not reasonably satisfied by the contractor, assignee, or licensees; or

(4) action is necessary because the agreement required by section 204 has not been obtained or waived or because a licensee of the exclusive right to use or sell any subject invention in the United States is in breach of its agreement obtained pursuant to section 204.

(b) A determination pursuant to this section or section 202(b)(4) shall not be subject to the Contract Disputes Act (41 U.S.C. Sec. 601 et seq.). An administrative appeals procedure shall be established by

附录 2 美国《拜杜法案》(Bayh – Dole Act, 1980)

regulations promulgated in accordance with section 206. Additionally, any contractor, inventor, assignee, or exclusive licensee adversely affected by a determination under this section may, at any time within sixty days after the determination is issued, file a petition in the United States Court of Federal Claims, which shall have jurisdiction to determine the appeal on the record and to affirm, reverse, remand or modify, as appropriate, the determination of the Federal agency. In cases described in paragraphs (1) and (3) of subsection (a), the agency's determination shall be held in abeyance pending the exhaustion of appeals or petitions filed under the preceding sentence.

– SOURCE –

(Added Pub. L. 96 – 517, Sec. 6(a), Dec. 12, 1980, 94 Stat. 3022; amended Pub. L. 98 – 620, title V, Sec. 501(9), Nov. 8, 1984, 98 Stat. 3367; Pub. L. 102 – 572, title IX, Sec. 902(b)(1), Oct. 29, 1992, 106 Stat. 4516; Pub. L. 107 – 273, div. C, title III, Sec. 13206(a)(14), Nov. 2, 2002, 116 Stat. 1905.)

– REFTEXT –

REFERENCES IN TEXT

The Contract Disputes Act of 1978, referred to in subsec. (b), is Pub. L. 95 – 563, Nov. 1, 1978, 92 Stat. 2383, as amended, which is classified principally to chapter 9 (Sec. 601 et seq.) of Title 41, Public Contracts. For complete classification of this Act to the Code see Short Title note set out under section 601 of Title 41 and Tables.

– MISC1 –

AMENDMENTS

2002 – Pub. L. 107-273 redesignated par. (1) as subsec. (a) and former subpars. (a) to (d) as pars. (1) to (4), respectively, redesignated former par. (2) as subsec. (b), struck out quotation marks and comma before "as appropriate", and substituted "paragraphs (1) and (3) of subsection (a)" for "paragraphs (a) and (c)".

1992 – Par. (2). Pub. L. 102-572 substituted "United States Court of Federal Claims" for "United States Claims Court".

1984 – Pub. L. 98-620 designated existing provisions as par. (1) and added par. (2).

EFFECTIVE DATE OF 1992 AMENDMENT

Amendment by Pub. L. 102-572 effective Oct. 29, 1992, see section 911 of Pub. L. 102-572, set out as a note under section 171 of Title 28, Judiciary and Judicial Procedure.

– End –

– CITE –

35 USC Sec. 204   01/03/05

– EXPCITE –

TITLE 35 – PATENTS

附录2　美国《拜杜法案》(Bayh – Dole Act, 1980)

PART II – PATENTABILITY OF INVENTIONS AND GRANT OF PATENTS

CHAPTER 18 – PATENT RIGHTS IN INVENTIONS MADE WITH FEDERAL ASSISTANCE

– HEAD –

Sec. 204. Preference for United States industry

– STATUTE –

Notwithstanding any other provision of this chapter, no small business firm or nonprofit organization which receives title to any subject invention and no assignee of any such small business firm or nonprofit organization shall grant to any person the exclusive right to use or sell any subject invention in the United States unless such person agrees that any products embodying the subject invention or produced through the use of the subject invention will be manufactured substantially in the United States. However, in individual cases, the requirement for such an agreement may be waived by the Federal agency under whose funding agreement the invention was made upon a showing by the small business firm, nonprofit organization, or assignee that reasonable but unsuccessful efforts have been made to grant licenses on similar terms to potential licensees that would be likely to manufacture substantially in the United States or that under the circumstances domestic manufacture is not commercially feasible.

- SOURCE -

(Added Pub. L. 96 - 517, Sec. 6(a), Dec. 12, 1980, 94 Stat. 3023.)

- End -

- CITE -

35 USC Sec. 205   01/03/05

- EXPCITE -

TITLE 35 - PATENTS

PART II - PATENTABILITY OF INVENTIONS AND GRANT OF PATENTS

CHAPTER 18 - PATENT RIGHTS IN INVENTIONS MADE WITH FEDERAL ASSISTANCE

- HEAD -

Sec. 205. Confidentiality

- STATUTE -

Federal agencies are authorized to withhold from disclosure to the public information disclosing any invention in which the Federal Government owns or may own a right, title, or interest (including a nonexclusive license) for a reasonable time in order for a patent application to be filed. Furthermore, Federal agencies shall not be required to release copies of any document which is part of an application for patent filed with the United States Patent and Trademark Office or with any foreign patent office.

– SOURCE –

(Added Pub. L. 96 – 517, Sec. 6(a), Dec. 12, 1980, 94 Stat. 3023.)

– End –

– CITE –

35 USC Sec. 206   01/03/05

– EXPCITE –

TITLE 35 – PATENTS
PART II – PATENTABILITY OF INVENTIONS AND GRANT OF PATENTS
CHAPTER 18 – PATENT RIGHTS IN INVENTIONS MADE WITH FEDERAL ASSISTANCE

– HEAD –

Sec. 206. Uniform clauses and regulations

– STATUTE –

The Secretary of Commerce may issue regulations which may be made applicable to Federal agencies implementing the provisions of sections 202 through 204 of this chapter and shall establish standard funding agreement provisions required under this chapter.

The regulations and the standard funding agreement shall be subject to public comment before their issuance.

– SOURCE –

(Added Pub. L. 96 – 517, Sec. 6(a), Dec. 12, 1980, 94 Stat. 3023; amended Pub. L. 98 – 620, title V, Sec. 501(10), Nov. 8, 1984, 98 Stat. 3367.)

– MISC1 –

AMENDMENTS

1984 – Pub. L. 98 – 620 amended section generally. Prior to amendment, section read as follows: "The Office of Federal Procurement Policy, after receiving recommendations of the Office of Science and Technology Policy, may issue regulations which may be made applicable to Federal agencies implementing the provisions of sections 202 through 204 of this chapter and the Office of Federal Procurement Policy shall establish standard funding agreement provisions required under this chapter."

– End –

– CITE –

35 USC Sec. 207

附录 2　美国《拜杜法案》(Bayh – Dole Act, 1980)

– EXPCITE –

TITLE 35 – PATENTS

PART II – PATENTABILITY OF INVENTIONS AND GRANT OF PATENTS

CHAPTER 18 – PATENT RIGHTS IN INVENTIONS MADE WITH FEDERAL ASSISTANCE

– HEAD –

Sec. 207. Domestic and foreign protection of federally owned inventions

– STATUTE –

(a) Each Federal agency is authorized to –

(1) apply for, obtain, and maintain patents or other forms of protection in the United States and in foreign countries on inventions in which the Federal Government owns a right, title, or interest;

(2) grant nonexclusive, exclusive, or partially exclusive licenses under federally owned inventions, royalty – free or for royalties or other consideration, and on such terms and conditions, including the grant to the licensee of the right of enforcement pursuant to the provisions of chapter 29 of this title as determined appropriate in the public interest;

(3) undertake all other suitable and necessary steps to protect and administer rights to federally owned inventions on behalf of the Federal Government either directly or through contract, including acquiring rights for and administering royalties to the Federal Government in any invention, but only to the extent the party from whom the rights are

acquired voluntarily enters into the transaction, to facilitate the licensing of a federally owned invention; and

(4) transfer custody and administration, in whole or in part, to another Federal agency, of the right, title, or interest in any federally owned invention.

(b) For the purpose of assuring the effective management of Government – owned inventions, the Secretary of Commerce is authorized to –

(1) assist Federal agency efforts to promote the licensing and utilization of Government – owned inventions;

(2) assist Federal agencies in seeking protection and maintaining inventions in foreign countries, including the payment of fees and costs connected therewith; and

(3) consult with and advise Federal agencies as to areas of science and technology research and development with potential for commercial utilization.

– SOURCE –

(Added Pub. L. 96 – 517, Sec. 6(a), Dec. 12, 1980, 94 Stat. 3023; amended Pub. L. 98 – 620, title V, Sec. 501(11), Nov. 8, 1984, 98 Stat. 3367; Pub. L. 106 – 404, Sec. 6(2), Nov. 1, 2000, 114 Stat. 1745.)

– MISC1 –

AMENDMENTS

2000 – Subsec. (a)(2). Pub. L. 106 – 404, Sec. 6(2)(A), substituted "inventions" for "patent applications, patents, or other

附录 2 美国《拜杜法案》(Bayh – Dole Act, 1980)

forms of protection obtained".

Subsec. (a)(3). Pub. L. 106 – 404, Sec. 6(2)(B), inserted, " including acquiring rights for and administering royalties to the Federal Government in any invention, but only to the extent the party from whom the rights are acquired voluntarily enters into the transaction, to facilitate the licensing of a federally owned invention" after "or through contract".

1984 – Pub. L. 98 – 620 designated existing provisions as subsec. (a) and added subsec. (b).

– EXEC –

EX. ORD. NO. 9424. ESTABLISHMENT OF A REGISTER OF GOVERNMENT INTERESTS IN PATENTS

Ex. Ord. No. 9424, Feb. 18, 1944, 9 F.R. 1959, provided:

1. The Secretary of Commerce shall cause to be established in the United States Patent Office [now Patent and Trademark Office] a separate register for the recording of all rights and interests of the Government in or under patents and applications for patents.

2. The several departments and other executive agencies of the Government, including Government – owned or Government – controlled corporations, shall forward promptly to the Commissioner of Patents [now Under Secretary of Commerce for Intellectual Property and Director of the United States Patent and Trademark Office] for recording in the separate register provided for in paragraph 1 hereof all licenses, assignments, or other interests of the Government in or under patents or applications for patents, in accordance with such rules and regulations as may be prescribed pursuant to paragraph 4 hereof; but

the lack of recordation in such register of any right or interest of the Government in or under any patent or application therefor shall not prejudice in any way the assertion of such right or interest by the Government.

3. The register shall be open to inspection except as to such entries or documents which, in the opinion of the department or agency submitting them for recording, should be maintained in secrecy: Provided, however, That the right of inspection may be restricted to authorized representatives of the Government pending the final report to the President by the National Patent Planning Commission under Executive Order No. 8977 of December 12, 1941, and action thereon by the President.

4. The Commissioner of Patents [now Under Secretary of Commerce for Intellectual Property and Director of the United States Patent and Trademark Office], with the approval of the Secretary of Commerce, shall prescribe such rules and regulations as he may deem necessary to effectuate the purposes of this order.

EX. ORD. NO. 9865. PATENT PROTECTION ABROAD OF INVENTIONS RESULTING FROM RESEARCH FINANCED BY THE GOVERNMENT

Ex. Ord. No. 9865, June 14, 1947, 12 F.R. 3907, as amended by Ex. Ord. No. 10096, Jan. 23, 1950, 15 F.R. 389, provided:

1. All Government departments and agencies shall, whenever practicable, acquire the right to file foreign patent applications on inventions resulting from research conducted or financed by the Government.

附录 2 美国《拜杜法案》(Bayh – Dole Act, 1980)

2. All Government departments and agencies which have or may hereafter acquire title to inventions or the right to file patent applications abroad thereon, shall fully and continuously inform the Chairman of Government Patents Board [now Secretary of Commerce. See Ex. Ord. No. 10930 set out as a note below] concerning such inventions, except as provided in section 6 hereof, and shall make recommendations to the Chairman of Government Patents Board as to which of such inventions should receive patent protection by the United States abroad and the foreign jurisdictions in which such patent protection should be sought. The recommendations of such departments and agencies shall indicate the immediate or future industrial, commercial or other value of the invention concerned, including its value to public health.

3. The Chairman of Government Patents Board shall determine whether, and in what foreign jurisdictions, the United States should seek patents for such inventions, and, to the extent of appropriations available therefor, shall procure patent protection for such inventions, taking all action, consistent with existing law, necessary to acquire and maintain patent rights abroad. Such determinations of the said Department shall be made after full consultation with United States industry and commerce, with the Department of State, and with other Government agencies familiar with the technical, scientific, industrial, commercial or other economic or social factors affecting the invention involved, and after consideration of the availability of valid patent protection in the countries determined to be immediate or potential markets for, or producers of, products, processes, or services covered by or relating to the invention.

4. The Chairman of Government Patents Board shall administer foreign patents acquired by the United States under the terms of this order and shall issue licenses thereunder in accordance with law under such rules and regulations as he shall prescribe. Nationals of the United States shall be granted licenses on a nonexclusive royalty free basis except in such cases as he shall determine and proclaim it to be inconsistent with the public interest to issue such licenses on a nonexclusive royalty free basis.

5. The Department of State, in consultation with the Chairman of Government Patents Board, shall negotiate arrangements among governments under which each government and its nationals shall have access to the foreign patents of the other participating governments. Patents relating to matters of public health may be licensed by the Chairman of Government Patents Board, with the approval of the Secretary of State, to any country or its nationals upon such terms and conditions as are in accordance with law and as the Chairman of Government Patents Board determines to be appropriate, regardless of whether such country is a party to the arrangements provided for in this section.

6. There shall be exempted from the provisions of this order (a) all inventions within the jurisdiction of the Atomic Energy Commission except in such cases as the said Commission specifically authorizes the inclusion of an invention under the terms of this order; and (b) all other inventions officially classified as secret or confidential for reasons of the national security. Nothing in this order shall supersede the declassification policies and procedures established by Executive Orders Nos. 9568 of June 8, 1945, 9604 of August 25, 1945, and 9809 of

附录 2 美国《拜杜法案》(Bayh – Dole Act, 1980)

December 12, 1946.

[Atomic Energy Commission abolished and all functions transferred to Administrator of Energy Research and Development Administration (unless otherwise specifically provided) by section 5814 of Title 42, The Public Health and Welfare. Energy Research and Development Administration terminated and functions vested by law in Administrator thereof transferred to Secretary of Energy (unless otherwise specifically provided) by sections 7151(a) and 7293 of Title 42.]

EX. ORD. NO. 10096. UNIFORM GOVERNMENT PATENT POLICY FOR INVENTIONS BY GOVERNMENT EMPLOYEES

Ex. Ord. No. 10096, Jan. 23, 1950, 15 F.R. 389, as amended by Ex. Ord. No. 10695, Jan. 16, 1957, 22 F.R. 365; Ex. Ord. No. 10930, Mar. 24, 1961, 26 F.R. 2583, provided:

NOW, THEREFORE, by virtue of the authority vested in me by the Constitution and statutes, and as President of the United States and Commander in Chief of the armed forces of the United States, in the interest of the establishment and operation of a uniform patent policy for the Government with respect to inventions made by Government employees, it is hereby ordered as follows:

1. The following basic policy is established for all Government agencies with respect to inventions hereafter made by any Government employee:

(a) The Government shall obtain the entire right, title, and interest in and to all inventions made by any Government employee (1) during working hours, or (2) with a contribution by the Government of facilities, equipment, materials, funds, or information, or of time or services of other Government employees on official duty, or (3) which bear a direct relation to or are made in consequence of the official duties of the inventor.

(b) In any case where the contribution of the Government, as measured by any one or more of the criteria set forth in paragraph (a) last above, to the invention, is insufficient equitably to justify a requirement of assignment to the Government of the entire right, title and interest to such invention, or in any case where the Government has insufficient interest in an invention to obtain entire right, title and interest therein (although the Government could obtain some under paragraph (a), above), the Government agency concerned, subject to the approval of the Chairman of the Government Patents Board [now Secretary of Commerce. See Ex. Ord. No. 10930 set out as a note below] (provided for in paragraph 3 of this order and hereinafter referred to as the Chairman), shall leave title to such invention in the employee, subject, however, to the reservation to the Government of a non – exclusive, irrevocable, royalty – free license in the invention with power to grant licenses for all governmental purposes, such reservation, in the terms thereof, to appear, where practicable, in any patent, domestic or foreign, which may issue on such invention.

(c) In applying the provisions of paragraphs (a) and (b), above, to the facts and circumstances relating to the making of any particular invention, it shall be presumed that an invention made by an employee who is employed or assigned (i) to invent or improve or perfect any art, machine, manufacture, or composition of matter, (ii) to conduct or perform research, development work, or both, (iii) to supervise,

附录2 美国《拜杜法案》(Bayh – Dole Act, 1980)

direct, coordinate, or review Government financed or conducted research, development work, or both, or (iv) to act in a liaison capacity among governmental or nongovernmental agencies or individuals engaged in such work, or made by an employee included within any other category of employees specified by regulations issued pursuant to section 4(b) hereof, falls within the provisions of paragraph (a), above, and it shall be presumed that any invention made by any other employee falls within the provisions of paragraph (b), above. Either presumption may be rebutted by the facts or circumstances attendant upon the conditions under which any particular invention is made and, not with standing the foregoing, shall not preclude a determination that the invention falls within the provisions of paragraph (d) next below.

(d) In any case wherein the Government neither (1) pursuant to the provisions of paragraph (a) above, obtains entire right, title and interest in and to an invention nor (2) pursuant to the provisions of paragraph (b) above, reserves a non – exclusive, irrevocable, royalty – free license in the invention with power to grant licenses for all governmental purposes, the Government shall leave the entire right, title and interest in and to the invention in the Government employee, subject to law.

(e) Actions taken, and rights acquired, under the foregoing provisions of this section, shall be reported to the Chairman in accordance with procedures established by him.

2. Subject to considerations of national security, or public health, safety, or welfare, the following basic policy is established for the collection, and dissemination to the public, of information concerning

inventions resulting from Government research and development activities:

(a) When an invention is made under circumstances defined in paragraph 1(a) of this order giving the United States the right to title thereto, the Government agency concerned shall either prepare and file an application for patent therefor in the United States Patent Office [now Patent and Trademark Office] or make a full disclosure of the invention promptly to the Chairman, who may, if he determines the Government interest so requires, cause application for patent to be filed or cause the invention to be fully disclosed by publication thereof: Provided, however, That, consistent with present practice of the Department of Agriculture, no application for patent shall, without the approval of the Secretary of Agriculture, be filed in respect of any variety of plant invented by any employee of that Department.

(b) [Revoked. Ex. Ord. No. 10695, Jan. 16, 1957, 22 F.R. 365]

3. (a) [Revoked. Ex. Ord. No. 10930, Mar. 24, 1961, 26 F.R. 2583]

(b) The Government Patents Board shall advise and confer with the Chairman concerning the operation of those aspects of the Government's patent policy which are affected by the provisions of this order or of Executive Order No. 9865 [set out above], and suggest modifications or improvements where necessary.

(c) [Revoked. Ex. Ord. No. 10930, Mar. 24, 1961, 26 F.R. 2583]

(d) The Chairman shall establish such committees and other working groups as may be required to advise or assist him in the performance of any of his functions.

附录2 美国《拜杜法案》(Bayh – Dole Act, 1980)

(e) The Chairman of the Government Patents Board and the Chairman of the Interdepartmental Committee on Scientific Research and Development (provided for by Executive Order No. 9912 of December 24, 1947), shall establish and maintain such mutual consultation as will effect the proper coordination of affairs of common concern.

4. With a view to obtaining uniform application of the policies set out in this order and uniform operations thereunder, the Chairman is authorized and directed:

(a) To consult and advise with Government agencies concerning the application and operation of the policies outlined herein;

(b) After consultation with the Government Patents Board, to formulate and submit to the President for approval such proposed rules and regulations as may be necessary or desirable to implement and effectuate the aforesaid policies, together with the recommendations of the Government Patents Board thereon;

(c) To submit annually a report to the President concerning the operation of such policies, and from time to time such recommendations for modification thereof as may be deemed desirable;

(d) To determine with finality any controversies or disputes between any Government agency and its employees, to the extent submitted by any party to the dispute, concerning the ownership of inventions made by such employees or rights therein; and

(e) To perform such other or further functions or duties as may from time to time be prescribed by the President or by statute.

5. The functions and duties of the Secretary of Commerce and the Department of Commerce under the provisions of Executive Order No.

9865 of June 14, 1947 [set out above] are hereby transferred to the Chairman and the whole or any part of such functions and duties may be delegated by him to any Government agency or officer: Provided, That said Executive Order No. 9865 shall not be deemed to be amended or affected by any provision of this Executive order other than this paragraph 5.

6. Each Government agency shall take all steps appropriate to effectuate this order, including the promulgation of necessary regulations which shall not be inconsistent with this order or with regulations issued pursuant to paragraph 4(b) hereof.

7. As used in this Executive order, the next stated terms, in singular and plural, are defined as follows for the purposes hereof:

(a) "Government agency" includes any executive department and any independent commission, board, office, agency, authority, or other establishment of the Executive Branch of the Government of the United States (including any such independent regulatory commission or board, any such wholly-owned corporation, and the Smithsonian Institution), but excludes the Atomic Energy Commission.

(b) "Government employee" includes any officer or employee, civilian or military, of any Government agency, except such part-time consultants or employees as may be excluded by regulations promulgated pursuant to paragraph 4(b) hereof.

(c) "Invention" includes any art, machine, manufacture, design, or composition of matter, or any new and useful improvement thereof, or any variety of plant, which is or may be patentable under the patent laws of the United States.

附录 2 美国《拜杜法案》(Bayh – Dole Act, 1980)

EX. ORD. NO. 10695. TRANSFER OF RECORDS TO DEPARTMENT OF COMMERCE

Section 2 of Ex. Ord. 10695, Jan. 16, 1957, 22 F.R. 365, provided that: "The Chairman of the Government Patents Board is hereby authorized to transfer to the Department of Commerce any or all of the records heretofore prepared by the Board pursuant to paragraph 2 (b) of Executive Order No. 10096 [set out above]."

EX. ORD. NO. 10930. ABOLITION OF GOVERNMENT PATENTS BOARD

Ex. Ord. No. 10930, Mar. 24, 1961, 26 F.R. 2583, provided:

By virtue of the authority vested in me as President of the United States, it is ordered as follows:

Section 1. The Government Patents Board, established by section 3 (a) of Executive Order No. 10096 of January 23, 1950 [set out above], and all positions established thereunder or pursuant thereto are hereby abolished.

Sec. 2. All functions of the Government Patents Board and of the Chairman thereof under the said Executive Order No. 10096, except the functions of conference and consultation between the Board and the Chairman, are hereby transferred to the Secretary of Commerce, who may provide for the performance of such transferred functions by such officer, employee, or agency of the Department of Commerce as he may designate.

Sec. 3. The Secretary of Commerce shall make such provision as may be necessary and consonant with law for the disposition or transfer of property, personnel, records, and funds of the Government Patents

Board.

Sec. 4. Except to the extent that they may be inconsistent with this order, all determinations, regulations, rules, rulings, orders, and other actions made or issued by the Government Patents Board, or by any Government agency with respect to any function transferred by this order, shall continue in full force and effect until amended, modified, or revoked by appropriate authority.

Sec. 5. Subsections (a) and (c) of section 3 of Executive Order No. 10096 are hereby revoked, and all other provisions of that order are hereby amended to the extent that they are inconsistent with the provisions of this order.

John F. Kennedy.

— End —

— CITE —

35 USC Sec. 208   01/03/05

— EXPCITE —

TITLE 35 — PATENTS

PART II — PATENTABILITY OF INVENTIONS AND GRANT OF PATENTS

CHAPTER 18 — PATENT RIGHTS IN INVENTIONS MADE WITH FEDERAL ASSISTANCE

— HEAD —

Sec. 208. Regulations governing Federal licensing

附录2　美国《拜杜法案》(Bayh-Dole Act, 1980)

- STATUTE -

The Secretary of Commerce is authorized to promulgate regulations specifying the terms and conditions upon which any federally owned invention, other than inventions owned by the Tennessee Valley Authority, may be licensed on a nonexclusive, partially exclusive, or exclusive basis.

- SOURCE -

(Added Pub. L. 96-517, Sec. 6(a), Dec. 12, 1980, 94 Stat. 3024; amended Pub. L. 98-620, title V, Sec. 501(12), Nov. 8, 1984, 98 Stat. 3367.)

- MISC1 -

AMENDMENTS

1984 - Pub. L. 98-620 substituted "Secretary of Commerce" for "Administrator of General Services".

- End -

- CITE -

35 USC Sec. 209　　　　　　　　　　　　　　　　01/03/05

- EXPCITE -

TITLE 35 - PATENTS

PART II - PATENTABILITY OF INVENTIONS AND GRANT OF

PATENTS

CHAPTER 18 – PATENT RIGHTS IN INVENTIONS MADE WITH FEDERAL ASSISTANCE

– HEAD –

Sec. 209. Licensing federally owned inventions

– STATUTE –

(a) Authority. – A Federal agency may grant an exclusive or partially exclusive license on a federally owned invention under section 207(a)(2) only if –

(1) granting the license is a reasonable and necessary incentive to –

(A) call forth the investment capital and expenditures needed to bring the invention to practical application; or

(B) otherwise promote the invention's utilization by the public;

(2) the Federal agency finds that the public will be served by the granting of the license, as indicated by the applicant's intentions, plans, and ability to bring the invention to practical application or otherwise promote the invention's utilization by the public, and that the proposed scope of exclusivity is not greater than reasonably necessary to provide the incentive for bringing the invention to practical application, as proposed by the applicant, or otherwise to promote the invention's utilization by the public;

(3) the applicant makes a commitment to achieve practical application of the invention within a reasonable time, which time may

附录 2 美国《拜杜法案》(Bayh-Dole Act, 1980)

be extended by the agency upon the applicant's request and the applicant's demonstration that the refusal of such extension would be unreasonable;

(4) granting the license will not tend to substantially lessen competition or create or maintain a violation of the Federal antitrust laws; and

(5) in the case of an invention covered by a foreign patent application or patent, the interests of the Federal Government or United States industry in foreign commerce will be enhanced.

(b) Manufacture in United States. – A Federal agency shall normally grant a license under section 207(a)(2) to use or sell any federally owned invention in the United States only to a licensee who agrees that any products embodying the invention or produced through the use of the invention will be manufactured substantially in the United States.

(c) Small Business. – First preference for the granting of any exclusive or partially exclusive licenses under section 207(a)(2) shall be given to small business firms having equal or greater likelihood as other applicants to bring the invention to practical application within a reasonable time.

(d) Terms and Conditions. – Any licenses granted under section 207(a)(2) shall contain such terms and conditions as the granting agency considers appropriate, and shall include provisions –

(1) retaining a nontransferrable, irrevocable, paid-up license for any Federal agency to practice the invention or have the invention practiced throughout the world by or on behalf of the Government of the United States;

(2) requiring periodic reporting on utilization of the invention, and utilization efforts, by the licensee, but only to the extent necessary to enable the Federal agency to determine whether the terms of the license are being complied with, except that any such report shall be treated by the Federal agency as commercial and financial information obtained from a person and privileged and confidential and not subject to disclosure under section 552 of title 5; and

(3) empowering the Federal agency to terminate the license in whole or in part if the agency determines that —

(A) the license is not executing its commitment to achieve practical application of the invention, including commitments contained in any plan submitted in support of its request for a license, and the license cannot otherwise demonstrate to the satisfaction of the Federal agency that it has taken, or can be expected to take within a reasonable time, effective steps to achieve practical application of the invention;

(B) the licensee is in breach of an agreement described in subsection (b);

(C) termination is necessary to meet requirements for public use specified by Federal regulations issued after the date of the license, and such requirements are not reasonably satisfied by the licensee; or

(D) the licensee has been found by a court of competent jurisdiction to have violated the Federal antitrust laws in connection with its performance under the license agreement.

(e) Public Notice. — No exclusive or partially exclusive license may be granted under section 207(a)(2) unless public notice of the intention to grant an exclusive or partially exclusive license on a federally owned invention has been provided in an appropriate manner at least 15 days before the license is granted, and the Federal agency has considered all comments received before the end of the comment period in response to that public notice. This subsection shall not apply to the licensing of inventions made under a cooperative research and development agreement entered into under section 12 of the Stevenson - Wydler Technology Innovation Act of 1980 (15 U.S.C. 3710a).

(f) Plan. - No Federal agency shall grant any license under a patent or patent application on a federally owned invention unless the person requesting the license has supplied the agency with a plan for development or marketing of the invention, except that any such plan shall be treated by the Federal agency as commercial and financial information obtained from a person and privileged and confidential and not subject to disclosure under section 552 of title 5.

- SOURCE -

(Added Pub. L. 96 - 517, Sec. 6(a), Dec. 12, 1980, 94 Stat. 3024; amended Pub. L. 106 - 404, Sec. 4(a), Nov. 1, 2000, 114 Stat. 1743; Pub. L. 107 - 273, div. C, title III, Sec. 13206(a) (15), Nov. 2, 2002, 116 Stat. 1905.)

- REFTEXT -

REFERENCES IN TEXT

The Federal antitrust laws, referred to in subsecs. (a)(4) and (d)(3)(D), are classified generally to chapter 1 (Sec. 1 et seq.) of Title 15, Commerce and Trade.

- MISC1 -

AMENDMENTS

2002 – Subsecs. (d)(2), (f). Pub. L. 107-273 struck out "of the United States Code" after "title 5".

2000 – Pub. L. 106-404 amended section catchline and text generally, restructuring and revising provisions setting forth criteria, terms, and conditions relating to granting of licenses on federally owned inventions.

- End -

- CITE -

35 USC Sec. 210   01/03/05

- EXPCITE -

TITLE 35 - PATENTS
PART II - PATENTABILITY OF INVENTIONS AND GRANT OF PATENTS
CHAPTER 18 - PATENT RIGHTS IN INVENTIONS MADE WITH FEDERAL ASSISTANCE

- HEAD -

Sec. 210. Precedence of chapter

附录2　美国《拜杜法案》(Bayh – Dole Act, 1980)

– STATUTE –

(a) This chapter shall take precedence over any other Act which would require a disposition of rights in subject inventions of small business firms or nonprofit organizations contractors in a manner that is inconsistent with this chapter, including but not necessarily limited to the following:

(1) section 10(a) of the Act of June 29, 1935, as added by title I of the Act of August 14, 1946 (7 U.S.C. 427i(a); 60 Stat. 1085);

(2) section 205(a) of the Act of August 14, 1946 (7 U.S.C. 1624 (a); 60 Stat. 1090);

(3) section 501(c) of the Federal Mine Safety and Health Act of 1977 (30 U.S.C. 951(c); 83 Stat. 742);

(4) section 30168(e) of title 49;

(5) section 12 of the National Science Foundation Act of 1950 (42 U.S.C. 1871(a); (!1)82 Stat. 360);

(6) section 152 of the Atomic Energy Act of 1954 (42 U.S.C. 2182; 68 Stat. 943);

(7) section 305 of the National Aeronautics and Space Act of 1958 (42 U.S.C. 2457);

(8) section 6 of the Coal Research Development Act of 1960 (30 U.S.C. 666; 74 Stat. 337);

(9) section 4 of the Helium Act Amendments of 1960 (50 U.S.C. 167b; 74 Stat. 920);

(10) section 32 of the Arms Control and Disarmament Act of 1961 (22 U.S.C. 2572; 75 Stat. 634);

(11) section 9 of the Federal Nonnuclear Energy Research and Development Act of 1974 (42 U.S.C. 5908; 88 Stat. 1878);

(12) section 5(d) of the Consumer Product Safety Act (15 U.S.C. 2054(d); 86 Stat. 1211);

(13) section 3 of the Act of April 5, 1944 (30 U.S.C. 323; 58 Stat. 191); (! 1)

(14) section 8001(c)(3) of the Solid Waste Disposal Act (42 U.S.C. 6981(c); 90 Stat. 2829);

(15) section 219 of the Foreign Assistance Act of 1961 (22 U.S.C. 2179; 83 Stat. 806);

(16) section 427(b) of the Federal Mine Health and Safety Act of 1977 (30 U.S.C. 937(b); 86 Stat. 155);

(17) section 306(d) of the Surface Mining and Reclamation Act of 1977 (30 U.S.C. 1226(d); 91 Stat. 455); (! 1)

(18) section 21(d) of the Federal Fire Prevention and Control Act of 1974 (15 U.S.C. 2218(d); 88 Stat. 1548);

(19) section 6(b) of the Solar Photovoltaic Energy Research Development and Demonstration Act of 1978 (42 U.S.C. 5585(b); 92 Stat. 2516);

(20) section 12 of the Native Latex Commercialization and Economic Development Act of 1978 (7 U.S.C. 178j; 92 Stat. 2533); and

(21) section 408 of the Water Resources and Development Act of 1978 (42 U.S.C. 7879; 92 Stat. 1360).

The Act creating this chapter shall be construed to take precedence over any future Act unless that Act specifically cites this Act and provides that it shall take precedence over this Act.

(b) Nothing in this chapter is intended to alter the effect of the laws cited in paragraph (a) of this section or any other laws with respect to

附录2 美国《拜杜法案》(Bayh – Dole Act, 1980)

the disposition of rights in inventions made in the performance of funding agreements with persons other than nonprofit organizations or small business firms.

(c) Nothing in this chapter is intended to limit the authority of agencies to agree to the disposition of rights in inventions made in the performance of work under funding agreements with persons other than nonprofit organizations or small business firms in accordance with the Statement of Government Patent Policy issued on February 18, 1983, agency regulations, or other applicable regulations or to otherwise limit the authority of agencies to allow such persons to retain ownership of inventions except that all funding agreements, including those with other than small business firms and nonprofit organizations, shall include the requirements established in section 202(c)(4) and section 203 of this title. Any disposition of rights in inventions made in accordance with the Statement or implementing regulations, including any disposition occurring before enactment of this section, are hereby authorized.

(d) Nothing in this chapter shall be construed to require the disclosure of intelligence sources or methods or to otherwise affect the authority granted to the Director of Central Intelligence by statute or Executive order for the protection of intelligence sources or methods.

(e) The provisions of the Stevenson – Wydler Technology Innovation Act of 1980 shall take precedence over the provisions of this chapter to the extent that they permit or require a disposition of rights in subject inventions which is inconsistent with this chapter.

- SOURCE -

(Added Pub. L. 96-517, Sec. 6(a), Dec. 12, 1980, 94 Stat. 3026; amended Pub. L. 98-620, title V, Sec. 501(13), Nov. 8, 1984, 98 Stat. 3367; Pub. L. 99-502, Sec. 9(c), Oct. 20, 1986, 100 Stat. 1796; Pub. L. 103-272, Sec. 5(j), July 5, 1994, 108 Stat. 1375; Pub. L. 104-113, Sec. 7, Mar. 7, 1996, 110 Stat. 779; Pub. L. 105-393, title II, Sec. 220(c)(2), Nov. 13, 1998, 112 Stat. 3625; Pub. L. 107-273, div. C, title III, Sec. 13206(a)(16), Nov. 2, 2002, 116 Stat. 1905.)

- REFTEXT -

REFERENCES IN TEXT

The Act and this Act, referred to in subsec. (a), is Pub. L. 96-517, Dec. 12, 1980, 94 Stat. 3015, which enacted sections 200 to 211 and 301 to 307 of this title, amended sections 41, 42, and 154 of this title, section 1113 of Title 15, Commerce and Trade, sections 101 and 117 of Title 17, Copyrights, and sections 2186, 2457, and 5908 of Title 42, The Public Health and Welfare, and enacted provisions set out as notes under sections 13 and 41 of this title. For complete classification of this Act to the Code, see Tables.

Section 12 of the National Science Foundation Act of 1950 (42 U.S.C. 1871(a); 82 Stat. 360), referred to in subsec. (a)(5), was amended by Pub. L. 99-159, title I, Sec. 109(c), Nov. 22, 1985, 99 Stat. 889, by striking out subsec. (b) and designating subsec. (a) as the entire section.

Section 3 of the Act of April 5, 1944 (30 U.S.C. 323; 58 Stat.

附录 2 美国《拜杜法案》（Bayh – Dole Act, 1980）

191), referred to in subsec. (a)(13), was omitted from the Code.

Section 306(d) of the Surface Mining and Reclamation Act, referred to in subsec. (a)(17), was classified to section 1226(d) of Title 30, Mineral Lands and Mining, prior to enactment of Pub. L. 98 – 409, which enacted a new section 1226 of Title 30. See section 1226(c) of Title 30.

The Native Latex Commercialization and Economic Development Act of 1978, referred to in subsec. (a)(20), is Pub. L. 95 – 592, Nov. 4, 1978, 92 Stat. 2529, as amended, which, as amended by Pub. L. 98 – 284, May 16, 1984, 98 Stat. 181, is known as the Critical Agricultural Materials Act and is classified principally to subchapter II (Sec. 178 et seq.) of chapter 8A of Title 7, Agriculture. For complete classification of this Act to the Code, see Short Title note set out under section 178 of Title 7 and Tables.

Section 408 of the Water Resources and Development Act of 1978 (42 U.S.C. 7879; 92 Stat. 1360), referred to in subsec. (a)(21), was repealed by Pub. L. 98 – 242, title I, Sec. 110(a), Mar. 22, 1984, 98 Stat. 101. See section 10308 of Title 42, The Public Health and Welfare.

The Stevenson – Wydler Technology Innovation Act of 1980, referred to in subsec. (e), is Pub. L. 96 – 480, Oct. 21, 1980, 94 Stat. 2311, as amended, which is classified generally to chapter 63 (Sec. 3701 et seq.) of Title 15, Commerce and Trade. For complete classification of this Act to the Code, see Short Title note set out under section 3701 of Title 15 and Tables.

– MISC1 –

AMENDMENTS

2002 – Subsec. (a)(11). Pub. L. 107–273, Sec. 13206(a)(16)(A)(i), substituted "5908" for "5901".

Subsec. (a)(20). Pub. L. 107–273, Sec. 13206(a)(16)(A)(ii), substituted "178j" for "178(j)".

Subsec. (c). Pub. L. 107–273, Sec. 13206(a)(16)(B), substituted "section 202(c)(4)" for "paragraph 202(c)(4)" and struck out second period after "title".

1998 – Subsec. (a)(11) to (22). Pub. L. 105–393 redesignated pars. (12) to (22) as (11) to (21), respectively, and struck out former par. (11) which read as follows: "subsection (e) of section 302 of the Appalachian Regional Development Act of 1965 (40 U.S.C. App. 302 (e); 79 Stat. 5);"

1996 – Subsec. (e). Pub. L. 104–113 struck out, "as amended by the Federal Technology Transfer Act of 1986," after "1980".

1994 – Subsec. (a)(4). Pub. L. 103–272 substituted "section 30168(e) of title 49" for "section 106(c) of the National Traffic and Motor Vehicle Safety Act of 1966 (15 U.S.C. 1395(c); 80 Stat. 721)".

1986 – Subsec. (e). Pub. L. 99–502 added subsec. (e).

1984 – Subsec. (c). Pub. L. 98–620 substituted "February 18, 1983" for "August 23, 1971 (36 Fed. Reg. 16887)" and inserted provision that all funding agreements, including those with other than small business firms and nonprofit organizations, shall include the requirements established in paragraph 202(c)(4) and section 203 of this title.

附录 2 美国《拜杜法案》(Bayh – Dole Act, 1980)

- CHANGE -

CHANGE OF NAME

Reference to the Director of Central Intelligence or the Director of the Central Intelligence Agency in the Director's capacity as the head of the intelligence community deemed to be a reference to the Director of National Intelligence. Reference to the Director of Central Intelligence or the Director of the Central Intelligence Agency in the Director's capacity as the head of the Central Intelligence Agency deemed to be a reference to the Director of the Central Intelligence Agency. See section 1081(a), (b) of Pub. L. 108 – 458, set out as a note under section 401 of Title 50, War and National Defense.

- FOOTNOTE -

(!1)See References in Text note below.

- End -

- CITE -

35 USC Sec. 211   01/03/05

- EXPCITE -

TITLE 35 – PATENTS
PART II – PATENTABILITY OF INVENTIONS AND GRANT OF

PATENTS
CHAPTER 18 – PATENT RIGHTS IN INVENTIONS MADE WITH FEDERAL ASSISTANCE

– HEAD –

Sec. 211. Relationship to antitrust laws

– STATUTE –

Nothing in this chapter shall be deemed to convey to any person immunity from civil or criminal liability, or to create any defenses to actions, under any antitrust law.

– SOURCE –

(Added Pub. L. 96 – 517, Sec. 6(a), Dec. 12, 1980, 94 Stat. 3027.)

– REFTEXT –

REFERENCES IN TEXT

The antitrust laws, referred to in text, are classified generally to chapter 1 (Sec. 1 et seq.) of Title 15, Commerce and Trade.

– End –

附录2 美国《拜杜法案》(Bayh – Dole Act, 1980)

– CITE –

35 USC Sec. 212   01/03/05

– EXPCITE –

TITLE 35 – PATENTS
PART II – PATENTABILITY OF INVENTIONS AND GRANT OF PATENTS
CHAPTER 18 – PATENT RIGHTS IN INVENTIONS MADE WITH FEDERAL ASSISTANCE

– HEAD –

Sec. 212. Disposition of rights in educational awards

– STATUTE –

No scholarship, fellowship, training grant, or other funding agreement made by a Federal agency primarily to an awardee for educational purposes will contain any provision giving the Federal agency any rights to inventions made by the awardee.

– SOURCE –

(Added Pub. L. 98 – 620, title V, Sec. 501(14), Nov. 8, 1984, 98 Stat. 3368.)

– End –

– CITE –

35 USC PART III – PATENTS AND PROTECTION OF PATENT RIGHTS   01/03/05

– EXPCITE –

TITLE 35 – PATENTS
PART III – PATENTS AND PROTECTION OF PATENT RIGHTS

– HEAD –

PART III – PATENTS AND PROTECTION OF PATENT RIGHTS

– MISC1 –

Chap.		Sec.
25.	Amendment and Correction of Patents	251
26.	Ownership and Assignment	261
27.	Government Interests in Patents	266
28.	Infringement of Patents	271
29.	Remedies for Infringement of Patent, and Other Actions	281
30.	Prior Art Citations to Office and Ex Parte Reexamination of Patents	301
31.	Optional Inter Partes Reexamination of Patents (! 1)	311

AMENDMENTS

2002 – Pub. L. 107 – 273, div. C, title III, Sec. 13206(a)(17), Nov. 2, 2002, 116 Stat. 1905, inserted a comma after

附录 2　美国《拜杜法案》(Bayh-Dole Act, 1980)

"Patent" in item for chapter 29.

1999 — Pub. L. 106-113, div. B, Sec. 1000(a)(9)[title IV, Sec. 4604(b)], Nov. 29, 1999, 113 Stat. 1536, 1501A-570, as amended by Pub. L. 107-273, div. C, title III, Sec. 13202(c)(2), Nov. 2, 2002, 116 Stat. 1902, substituted "Ex Parte Reexamination of Patents" for "Reexamination of Patents" in item for chapter 30 and added item for chapter 31.

1982 — Pub. L. 97-256, title I, Sec. 101(7), Sept. 8, 1982, 96 Stat. 816, added item for chapter 30.

- FOOTNOTE -

(！1) So in original. Does not conform to chapter heading.

- End -